GEORGE ELIOT

A BEGINNER'S GUIDE

JENNY WEATHERBURN

Series Editors
Rob Abbott & Charlie Bell

Hodder & Stoughton
A MEMBER OF THE HODDER HEADLINE GROUP

Orders: please contact Bookpoint Ltd, 130 Milton Park, Abingdon, Oxon OX14 4SB. Telephone: (44) 01235 827720, Fax: (44) 01235 400554. Lines are open from 9.00–6.00, Monday to Saturday, with a 24-hour message answering service. Email address: orders@bookpoint.co.uk

British Library Cataloguing in Publication Data
A catalogue record for this title is available from The British Library

ISBN 0 340 85731 5

First published 2002
Impression number   10 9 8 7 6 5 4 3 2 1
Year   2007 2006 2005 2004 2003 2002

Copyright © 2003 Jenny Weatherburn

Cover photo from Bettman/Corbis.
Typeset by Transet Limited, Coventry, England.
Printed in Great Britain for Hodder & Stoughton Educational, a division of Hodder Headline Plc, 338 Euston Road, London NW1 3BH by Cox & Wyman, Reading, Berks.

CONTENTS

How to use this book

The *Beginner's Guide* series aims to introduce readers to major writers of the past 500 years. It is assumed that readers will begin with little or no knowledge and will want to go on to explore the subject in other ways.

BEGIN READING THE AUTHOR

This book is a companion guide to George Eliot's major works; it is not a substitute for reading the books themselves. It would be useful if you read some of the works in parallel, so that you can put theory into practice. This book is divided into sections. After considering how to approach the author's work and a brief biography, we go on to explore some of Eliot's main writings and themes before examining some critical approaches to the author. The survey finishes with suggestions for further reading and possible areas of further study.

HOW TO APPROACH UNFAMILIAR OR DIFFICULT TEXTS

Coming across a new writer may seem daunting, but do not be put off. The trick is to persevere.

Literary work often needs to be read more than once, and in different ways. These ways can include: a leisurely and superficial reading to get the main ideas and narrative; a slower, more detailed reading, focusing on the nuances of the text, concentrating on what appear to be key passages; and reading in a random way, moving back and forth through the text to examine such things as themes, narrative or characterization.

VOCABULARY

You will see that keywords and unfamiliar words are set in **bold** text. These words are defined and explained in the glossary to be found at the back of the book.

This book is a tool to help you appreciate a key figure in literature. We hope you enjoy reading it and find it useful.

---

* * *SUMMARY * * *

To maximize the use of this book:

- read the author's work;

- read it several times in different ways;

- be open to innovative or unusual forms of writing;

- persevere.

Rob Abbott and Charlie Bell
Series Editors

Why Read Eliot Today?

When the majority of readers open a new novel today they anticipate finding a galaxy of convincing characters in whom they can believe, including several with whom they can empathize. Victorian readers had no such expectations – why should they have had? Available reading matter did not, on the whole, provide them with this experience. Eliot was one of the first to change these expectations; she is so very interesting because she is one of the first 'modern' novelists in this respect.

Eliot's work has had a huge influence on later writers. It has provided a model to follow, to develop, and to react against. Of the inheritors, Henry James's *Portrait of a Lady* was very directly inspired by *Daniel Deronda*. Elaine Showalter, in her paper 'The Greening of Sister George' (*Nineteenth-Century Fiction*, 1980) includes Simone de Beauvoir, P. D. James and Margaret Drabble in her list of eminent women writers who are indebted to Eliot. Margaret Drabble's *The Waterfall* has interesting parallels of plot and character with *The Mill on the Floss*.

However, one of the differences between *The Mill on the Floss* and its inheritor, *The Waterfall* – the fact that Jane (Maggie) gets her man – highlights one of the favourite criticisms of Eliot: her heroines are never allowed the same kind of interesting, independent lives in their fictional worlds as Eliot herself enjoyed in her real one. Eliot is a deeply admired and respected writer, *Middlemarch* being in the eyes of many 'the' representative Victorian text, but she has attracted some challenging and acerbic criticism.

A CHARITABLE WORLD VIEW

Characters

It is ironic that Eliot, who is remarkable not only for the plethora of believable characters who people her novels, but for the charity, tolerance, understanding and subtlety that she brings to these characters, should have been beset by such a degree of sharply unsympathetic criticism. Eliot's unusually fair approach can be demonstrated by looking at a standard situation: two women attracted to the same man – and examining how Eliot and two comparable, and excellent, women writers, Jane Austen and Charlotte Brontë, deal with it.

Jane Austen died two years before Eliot was born. Her famous novel, *Pride and Prejudice*, published in 1813, deals with the uncertain progress of the romance between the heroine, Elizabeth Bennett, and Darcy.

Charlotte Brontë was three years older than Eliot. Her best known novel, *Jane Eyre*, was published in 1847; this follows another troubled romance between the heroine of the title and Rochester.

In both these novels there is a beautiful, well-bred competitor for the gentleman in question: Miss Bingley in *Pride and Prejudice* and Blanche Ingram in *Jane Eyre*. As readers, we are not invited to take these rivals seriously; we are rather encouraged to identify with the heroine's viewpoint and to ridicule their shallowness, transparent manoeuvring, rudeness and ill-judged complacency. This can be seen as a cheap trick on the part of the novelists and appeals to the lowest common denominator in human nature. We all love to feel superior; we are all tempted to join in when people we admire are sneering at others. Neither Austen nor Brontë invites us to see things from the rivals' viewpoint and share in their inevitable deep disappointments and misery: the situation is simplified and rendered one-sided.

Contrast their approach with Eliot's in *The Mill on the Floss*, which was published in 1860. The love interest between Maggie Tulliver and Stephen Guest is scarcely the mainspring of the novel but it is a crucial element in the latter part – and long before reaching this we have closely identified ourselves with Maggie's point of view. However, Stephen is already engaged to Maggie's cousin, Lucy Deane who, with her exquisite china-doll perfection, has long been the invidious comparison blighting Maggie's young life. Eliot does not take up Charlotte Brontë's stance (and this was another plain woman writing) of wreaking revenge on the beautiful rival by sneering at her and making her an object of ridicule. Maggie loves and respects her cousin – and as readers we do too; we see Lucy's point of view as well as Maggie's. And when Maggie chooses not to have Stephen when he could have been hers for the asking, we feel and appreciate all the subtle complexities of the situation – as in real life.

And beyond

A benevolent tolerance and wisdom imbues Eliot's novels. The author guides us, the reader, and dispenses advice en route. At first this may be difficult for a modern reader to get used to: one cannot imagine a current writer having the same temerity or certainty of purpose. However, once you are used to it, it is strangely comforting – you can pick up a novel like *Middlemarch* knowing that it will not only entertain but remind you of well-expressed eternal truths. Here is the opening to Chapter 55:

> If youth is the season of hope, it is often so only in the sense that our elders are hopeful about us: for no age is so apt as youth to think its emotions, partings, and resolves are the last of their kind. Each crisis seems final, simply because it is new.

This is sometimes done through a character's words or thoughts rather than direct authorial intervention. In *Middlemarch*, when confronting a wealth of 'personal cares', Lydgate reflects on the value of the 'beneficent harness of routine' which helps to keep him sane in the crisis. In *Daniel Deronda*, Daniel responds to Gwendolen's complaint about boredom with the tactful generalization: 'I think what we call dullness of things is a disease in ourselves.'

HUMOUR

Some of Eliot's characters are incredibly funny, hugely enjoyable and quite unforgettable. Mrs Poyser, in *Adam Bede*, is a reliable source of the pithy and the down-to-earth; she has been a favourite since first publication of the novel: it is worth reading for her alone. Who could forget her reaction to the grand celebrations for Arthur Donnithorne's twenty-first birthday? As they are leaving the party, she says to her husband:

> 'I'd sooner ha' brewin' day and washin' day together than one o' these pleasurin' days. There's no work so tirin' as danglin' about an' starin' an' not rightly knowin' what you're goin' to do next; and keepin' your face i' smilin' order like a grocer o' market-day for fear people shouldna think you civil enough. An' you've nothing to show for't when it's done, if it isn't a yellow face wi' eatin' things as disagree. (Ch. 24)

Lydgate reflects on the value of the 'beneficent harness of routine'.

The Mill on the Floss brings us the inimitable Dodson sisters. There is the famously ghastly Mrs Glegg and her sister, Mrs Pullet, who combines an apparently fervid concern with other people's health and a fanatically house-proud outlook with her sister's sense of the importance of preserving certain things for best. In Book 1, Chapter 9, she takes her sister, Mrs Tulliver, Mrs Tulliver's two children and their cousin on a ceremonial visit to her best bonnet. This has all the aspect of religious fervour and takes quite some time. They have to first go to collect a door key, hidden in one wardrobe, before processing to another part of the house where this can be used to unlock a room housing yet another wardrobe, in the depths of which is eventually revealed the bonnet. Its revelation, after such a performance, is quite 'an anticlimax to Maggie, who would have preferred something more strikingly preternatural'.

ELIOT'S LANGUAGE

Eliot was an outstandingly intelligent woman who loved language and had a sensuous appreciation of its possibilities. In November, 1841, she wrote to Maria Lewis: 'I love words; they are the quoits, the bows, the staves that furnish the gymnasium of the mind', Vol. 1, *The George Eliot Letters*, ed. Gordon S. Haight (New Haven, 1954–78). To read Eliot at her best is to be given the opportunity to revel in her ability to deploy the best words in the best order. This can be in the slightest of descriptions – her encapsulation of one of the most minor of characters (Miss Morgan, the Vincys' governess in *Middlemarch*) in four words: 'brown, dull and resigned' – or the most complex metaphorical passages. Eliot's use of metaphorical language has attracted a good deal of critical commentary; views which we will take into consideration later in this volume.

* * *SUMMARY* * *

Read Eliot for:

- the understanding it gives you of her influence in novel writing;

- the subtlety of her characterization;

- the charity and wisdom of her world view;

- her sense of humour;

- her use of language.

Biography and Influences

2

A WORD ABOUT NAMES

Unusually, in the case of this author, it is the pen name 'George Eliot' which identifies her and which people remember. In fact it only came into being in 1857 when a plausible persona was required for the publisher of her first novel. During her life she changed her signature with disconcerting regularity. These alterations will be traced in this chapter, after which we will settle for the simplicity of the pseudonym.

EARLY LIFE

Industrial and rural influences

George Eliot was born Mary Anne Evans on 22nd November 1819 in Warwickshire, the youngest child of her father's second marriage. Her father, Robert Evans, was agent for the owner of Arbury Hall. Mary Anne grew up loving both the countryside and her older brother Isaac who was her best friend and companion: this childhood experience was drawn on in *The Mill on the Floss*. The whole family were involved in the rhythms of agriculture: her mother's pride and joy was the dairy, which she presided over with as much care and dedication as Mrs Poyser in *Adam Bede* or Priscilla Lammeter in *Silas Marner*.

Mary Anne not only visited Arbury Hall and the cottages of farm labourers with her father but also followed him into miners' cottages and recognized the striking physical differences between miners, or those involved in cottage industries like the handloom weavers, compared to more stalwart farm folk. She was an acute observer of the very varied habits of dress and speech that she encountered – all of which she would later use in her novels.

An over-sensitive and needy child

Mary Anne's childhood was happy but not perfect. Her father was both formidable and exacting. She idolized her brother – who was fond of her but failed to reciprocate her affection with like intensity. As soon as Isaac acquired a pony at the age of about nine, he left Mary Anne, hitherto his constant companion, to her own devices. His abandonment caused his sister enormous grief and trauma.

His abandonment caused his sister enormous grief and trauma.

Isaac was his mother's favourite child. Whilst fond of Mary Anne, she appears to have shown her affection inconsistently, occasionally making much of the child but more often making it apparent that she found her tiresome, demanding and altogether a far from ideal small daughter. This seems to have created a vicious circle: the sensitive, needy Mary Anne responded by being even more demanding and attention-seeking – which resulted in more rejection. There are decided echoes of this in *The Mill on the Floss*. The child's sense of rejection must have been accentuated by the decision to send her to boarding school at the tender age of five.

An over-sensitive and needy young woman

As a consequence of her childhood, Mary Anne was demanding and needy of affection all her life. Her insecurity and deep unhappiness with herself as a young woman were shown in her occasional outbursts of hysterical tears – usually during concerts – which succeeded in embarrassing everyone. At this time she searched for and found a substitute for the deep uncritical maternal love which she had so desperately needed – but been deprived of – in a series of intense friendships with other women. Her close friendship with Sara Hennell is a good example. A little later she moved on to a series of heterosexual relationships, often with older, inappropriate and unavailable men. The pattern of these relationships was initial intellectual engagement followed first by an all-absorbing passionate commitment – at least on her side – then by embarrassed withdrawal. She remained plagued by self-doubt and painfully vulnerable to criticism. She was often unwell.

Religion

Mary Anne tried the standard Victorian consolation of devoting herself to religion, at least for a time. In a way this can be seen as beginning when she was first sent away to school. Like many children, she made the simplistic assumption that she had been sent away from her beloved home because she had been intolerably naughty; she therefore set about being good. By the time she was about twenty – occasional hysterical outbursts aside – she appeared a dour, disapproving and devout Evangelical Anglican. She even dropped the final 'e' from her second name in 1837, presumably because the form with which she had been christened had Catholic connotations.

However, in 1841, Mary Ann made the acquaintance of a group of freethinkers in Coventry and her religious belief, which had been weakened in any case by her wider reading in science and philosophy, vanished entirely. As a consequence, she refused to attend church with her father in the January of 1842. This rigid attitude – as extreme as her previous religious stance had been – did not last long. By May of the same year she accompanied her father to church once more. This was not the result of hypocritical compromise, more the beginning of a balanced, tolerant and truly charitable world view, one of her most attractive attributes.

INDEPENDENCE AND THE *WESTMINSTER REVIEW*

When she was 30, Mary Ann took her first steps towards independence: travelling abroad with friends, staying alone in Geneva, doing some translation work. Her translation of Strauss's *Leben Jesu* influenced the thinking of many English readers. However, her move to London in 1851 to work on the *Westminster Review* can perhaps be seen as a truly independent, and unusual, step. It was also one which was going to both influence her novel writing and provide a medium for introduction to George Henry Lewes.

Marian – she had decided this new phase of her life merited a more unusual and modern form of her name – arrived in London in January 1851. Initially she stayed with John Chapman, publisher, bookseller, provider of an avant-garde guest house and editor of the *Westminster Review*. After an initial sexual dalliance with Chapman, another wholly unsuitable candidate – he was already living in a *menage à trois* with his wife and the governess of his children – Marian agreed to stay on seemingly humiliating terms which nevertheless suited them both well. She would accept free board and lodging without sex (the household had proved intolerably stormy while Chapman was attempting to satisfy three women, all occupying the same premises) and would be the unofficial assistant editor of the *Westminster Review*.

Marian, uncredited, ran the *Westminster Review* for ten numbers of that journal and in doing so came into contact with some of the finest minds in Europe and Britain. She re-established it as the leading intellectual quarterly of the day – but perhaps an even more notable achievement was that she established herself as a real intellectual and professional success: a lone woman working in a man's world. During her two years working on the *Westminster Review*, Marian read and reviewed some 166 books, many of them works of fiction. This intense immersion in contemporary literature enabled her to clarify her ideas about what she felt was successful and what was not: this would be invaluable when she later started to write fiction herself.

CONSCIOUS OF HER LOOKS

Any woman, born into any era or culture, is handicapped if her looks do not suit the prevailing fashion. This state of affairs is even worse for the morbidly sensitive. Marian had a long face, heavy jaw, big mouth and large nose. 'Equine', as used by Henry James in a letter (to William James, 1 May 1878, Vol. 2, *Letters of Henry James*, ed. Leon Edel, p. 72) seems to have been one of the kinder words which sprang to mind on first seeing her. Her features struck many as being masculine rather than feminine; Emily Tennyson commented particularly on the apparent dichotomy between her voice and her features when she met her in 1871: 'She speaks in a soft soprano voice, which almost sounds like a fine falsetto with her strong, masculine face', quoted in *Emily Tennyson: The Poet's Wife* by Ann Thwaite (faber & faber, 1996).

Of course Marian's charisma, kindness, witty intelligence – and above all her capacity for attentive listening – went a long way to offset any initial adverse impression which her looks might have established. Presumably she cared less about such things as she got older. However, in her youth at any rate, her appearance must have influenced Marian's self-image and made her question whether she would ever maintain a successful relationship with a man.

GEORGE HENRY LEWES

A superficially unsuitable suitor

George Henry Lewes, who must at first have seemed another in the long line of unsuitable/unavailable men as he was already married, was, perhaps mercifully, considered relatively unattractive himself. Lewes had married Agnes Jervis in 1841. By the time he started a relationship with Marian in 1852, he had three sons by Agnes. However, their marriage effectively ended in 1849 when Agnes embarked on what was to be a long-term liaison with one Thornton Hunt. In 1850 she gave birth to Hunt's son – the first of several children by him – and Lewes registered the child as his own. Later this may have given him cause for regret, because by giving the child his name, Lewes was, by the laws of the time, condoning his wife's adultery and giving up any future right to sue for divorce.

Thus when Marian left to live abroad with Lewes for a time in 1854 she was making an extraordinarily brave decision. As a consequence of Victorian double standards, living with a man to whom one was not married more or less put the woman outside acceptable Victorian society, although it did not harm the man's reputation. Moreover, there was no guarantee that Lewes would indeed leave Agnes permanently and live with Marian. If he did not, no particular shame would attach itself to Lewes, but for Marian it would mean a life of permanent social exclusion. Moreover, she must have known that her brother Isaac, who still meant a great deal to her, would react violently against such apparent family disgrace.

A devoted partnership

However, this apparently chancy endeavour turned out to be one of the biggest successes of Marian's life. Lewes was a talented, successful and secure intellectual who never felt threatened by Marian's fame. He was also a lively and entertaining man who, in Kathryn Hughes' splendid wording, was able to provide 'the crucial airy counter-balance to her marshy gloom', *George Eliot* (Fourth Estate, 1998). She and Lewes adored each other: they were completely sexually, emotionally and intellectually compatible; he remained her support and bastion against the world until his death. His role as her protector was in one way a disadvantage because, by shielding her from any adverse reviews, he prevented her from taking these remarks into account as she continued to write. However, the security of absolute unconditional love helped her to become less neurotic; he encouraged her to start writing her novels and to continue when she found it a struggle. Her dedication to him at the beginning of the manuscript of *Felix Holt* says it all:

> From George Eliot (otherwise Polly) to her dear husband, this thirteenth year of their united life, in which the deepening sense of her own imperfectness has the consolation of their deepening love.

Lewes' pet name for Marian was Polly; she insisted on being called 'Mrs Lewes' during their 24-year-long relationship, although they were, in fact, never married.

Lewes died in 1878; Marian married John Cross, twenty years her junior, a man who she had known for years, in May 1880. She clearly needed the affection and security of a relationship. A rather pathetic line from one of her letters to Cross reads: 'the sun shines so cold, so cold, when there are no eyes to look love on me'. This relationship did not endure as Marian died in the December of the year she was married.

✳ ✳ ✳ SUMMARY ✳ ✳ ✳

The key influences on Eliot as a writer were:

- her childhood in Warwickshire, which gave her the opportunity to observe customs, accents and types of people;

- her family relationships;

- her formidable intellect and plain looks;

- the period she spent working on the *Westminster Review*;

- her relationship with George Henry Lewes.

3 The Victorian Moral Scene

Eliot can be seen as solidly Victorian: she was born only six months later than Queen Victoria, although she died some twenty years before her. Although typically Victorian in some ways, in others Eliot seems daringly modern. She seemed something of a contradiction even to her contemporaries: Henry James wrote in a review published in the *Atlantic Monthly* of May 1885:

> What is remarkable, extraordinary – and the process remains inscrutable and mysterious – is that this quiet, anxious, sedentary, serious, invalidical English lady, without animal spirits, without adventures, without extravagance, assumption, or bravado, should have made us believe that nothing in the world was alien to her; should have produced such rich, deep, masterly pictures of the multifold life of man.

Because at first glance Eliot's attitudes and lifestyle appear to contain inherent contradictions, it is worth trying to understand the forces at work here.

MEN, WOMEN AND WORK

In the Victorian period, men and women were regarded as being completely different in absolutely every respect. This was a view of uncompromising polarity: masculine characteristics belonged to men and feminine ones to women – with no overlap. As far as the middle classes were concerned, university education and careers belonged to men; this meant work and leadership in industry, politics, law, religion; whilst supervision of children and the home was left to the 'weaker' sex. Women of the lower classes worked of course, which meant that the simple fact of a lady's employment was a demonstration of her embarrassing lack of means. This explains Gwendolen's horror and distaste at the thought that she might have to become a governess in

Daniel Deronda. Another heroine, Maggie Tulliver in *The Mill on the Floss*, works in 'a third-rate schoolroom', and hates it, when she needs to earn money. This, together with setting up a school, was a kind of employment acceptable for those middle-class women fallen on hard times. The only other respectable alternative for a lady in straitened circumstances was sewing, like Mrs Meyrick and her daughters in *Daniel Deronda*.

Writing was not regarded as a career for women, more a kind of self-indulgent hobby. Jane Austen, who died two years before Eliot's birth, and Mrs Gaskell, Eliot's contemporary, wrote under their own names and achieved success. But they did not, on the whole, desperately need the money: Austen was kept by her brother and Gaskell by her husband. Another set of contemporaries, the Brontë sisters, did indeed need the money and saw any alternative as preferable to the detested role of governess. Like Eliot, the Brontë sisters wrote under pseudonyms in order to get published in the first place; however, they remained in relative isolation at Haworth. Charlotte Brontë ventured from home more often and worked abroad, but she was nervous and ill at ease on the few occasions she visited London.

George Eliot

Contrast this with Eliot: a resounding success in a man's world. Like the Brontës, she aimed to avoid governessing as a means of earning money, like Charlotte she was rather plain; unlike them she became accepted into the (masculine) intellectual elite of her day. During her lifetime Eliot knew and/or corresponded with not only other writers such as Dickens, Thackeray and Carlyle but with poets (Tennyson, Robert Browning, Ralph Waldo Emerson), scientists (Charles Darwin, Herbert Spencer), artists (Edward Burne-Jones, Frederic Lehmann), and composers (Liszt and Wagner). There are several examples of this extraordinary achievement; one is the often quoted anecdote of Bessie Belloc:

I can see her descending the great staircase of our house in Savile Row ...
on my father's arm, the only lady, except my mother, among the group
of remarkable men, politicians and authors of the first literary rank.
(Bessie R. Belloc, 'Dorothea Casaubon and George Eliot' *Contemporary
Review*, Feb. 1894).

Eliot was probably happiest and most confident in this sort of milieu
rather than one in which she was competing with other women.

Despite the fact that Eliot earned her own living so successfully by
own efforts, this was not a course which she recommended for others,
either in real life or through her fiction. She did not see the point of
women, or working-class men, having the vote until they were better
educated – and she saw education as enabling women to become more
intelligent and thoughtful wives and mothers rather than allowing
them to enter paid employment. Feminists have objected to the small-
scale successes and low-key endings for women in her novels: Dinah
gives up preaching to become a devoted wife and mother in *Adam Bede*

and Dorothea, after such promise, is similarly restricted in *Middlemarch*. However, it is only fair to surmise that Eliot, such a sharply intelligent woman, must have resented, at least occasionally, the very different Victorian expectations of and opportunities for men and women. There is a flash of this in *Daniel Deronda* when Daniel's mother says to him, 'you can never imagine what it is to have a man's force of genius in you, and yet to suffer the slavery of being a girl'. In *The Mill on the Floss*, Maggie too is driven to 'wish I could make myself a world outside it [domesticity and family], as men do'.

MEN, WOMEN AND SEX

Nowadays, Victorian society appears to us repressed and hypocritical in its attitudes towards sex. A man's reputation was, if anything, enhanced by sexual dalliance. No particular odium attaches to Grandcourt in *Daniel Deronda* for having a long-term relationship with Lydia Glasher, another man's wife, and having four children by her. When Grandcourt announces to Lydia that he wishes to end their relationship and marry Gwendolen, Lydia recognizes at once that 'he would go scathless, it was she who had to suffer'. In this she is entirely accurate, because of her past she becomes 'a woman destitute of acknowledged social dignity'.

A woman's reputation, however, was not only completely ruined by any taint of less than conventional sexual behaviour, but also any misdemeanour was always regarded as being entirely her fault. Maggie has only to disappear fleetingly with Stephen Guest and, although no intimacy takes place, public opinion is absolutely uncompromising. Eliot remarks cynically:

> If Miss Tulliver, after a few months of well-chosen travel, had returned as Mrs Stephen Guest – with a post-marital trousseau, and all the advantages possessed by even the most unwelcome wife of an only son, public opinion, which at St Ogg's, as elsewhere, always knew what to think, would have judged in strict consistency with those results.' (*The Mill on the Floss*, Book 7, Chapter 2)

But in the prevailing circumstances, 'society saw at once that Miss Tulliver's conduct had been of the most aggravated kind'. However, 'as for poor Mr Stephen Guest, he was rather pitiable than otherwise; a young man of five-and-twenty is not to be too severely judged in these cases – he is really very much at the mercy of a designing bold girl'.

George Eliot

In terms of morals too, Eliot's life was ambiguous. On the one hand, she was regarded by her adoring fans as a secure moral guide in a time when religious faith was beginning to weaken and social mores were changing. Bernard Semmel, in *George Eliot and the Politics of National Inheritance* (Oxford University Press, 1994) makes this point and quotes G.M. Young's assertion that she 'saved us from the moral catastrophe which might have been expected to follow upon the waning of religious conviction'(*Victorian England: Portrait of an Age*, Oxford University Press, 1936). On the other hand, this is a woman whose husband, John Cross, was refused permission to bury her in Poet's Corner in Westminster Abbey even though the Dean had been a personal friend of the Leweses. Whilst this was partly because of the doubts that she had expressed over Christian belief, it was mainly because she had chosen to live in sin for so long with Lewes.

Once Eliot moved in with Lewes, she (but not he) was ostracized by polite English society. Her brother Isaac considered her disgraced, did not contact her again for many years, and forbade their two half-sisters to communicate with her. Eliot was forced to adopt the pseudonym in order to get her first novel, *Scenes of Clerical Life*, published: there would have been no hope of its success had readers known at the time that the author was, in fact, the scandalous Marian Evans. Once her pseudonym was rumbled, in 1860, Eliot and Lewes fled to Italy on publication of *The Mill on the Floss* in order to avoid any unsavoury publicity. Fortunately, by then *Adam Bede* had been so very much enjoyed that any novel by the same author was well received, regardless of Eliot's clearly deplorable morals. By the mid 1860s, Eliot's phenomenal success had effected a miraculous change in suburban English attitudes and she was regarded as being almost acceptable.

Despite what appears to be brave and unconventional personal behaviour of her own, Eliot held conventional beliefs on marriage. She firmly believed in it as an institution and regarded herself as morally married to Lewes. They referred to themselves as married and called themselves Mr and Mrs Lewes. Eliot felt no inclination to keep her maiden name as a kind of principle and rebuked those who continued to address her by it once she was living with Lewes.

Eliot was a woman of strong principles who chose to live flexibly in a way which suited her, rather than in accordance with conventional rules. Nevertheless, this did not make for an easy life: the consequent conflict, unresolved tensions and guilt are dealt with in Sandra M. Gilbert and Susan Gubar's *The Madwoman in the Attic* (Yale University Press, 1979).

✳ ✳ ✳ SUMMARY ✳ ✳ ✳

- Victorians held strong views as to what was appropriate behaviour for men and women.

- Whilst Eliot took the unconventional course of working for her living, she held the conventional view that women should remain in the home as wives and mothers.

- Similarly, whilst her choice to live with Lewes out of wedlock was unconventional, she regarded and presented herself as conventionally married to him.

4 How to Approach Eliot's Work

Whether you are new to Eliot, or returning to her novels to consider them in greater depth, you are in for a treat. You may find it helpful to bear the following features of her writing in mind before beginning.

There are three characteristic aspects of Eliot's novels that will not surprise a modern reader, although they were unusual in her own time. One is that they often include descriptions of people working – like Adam in his carpentry shop (*Adam Bede*) or Silas weaving (*Silas Marner*). The second is that she is as much interested in relationships between older couples as in those involving young love. The third is her sensitive depiction of children.

SETTING
Apart from *Romola*, Eliot's novels are set wholly or largely in provincial rural England. With the one exception of *Daniel Deronda*, which is set in the near present, they are located forty to sixty years in the past. This historical perspective gave Eliot several advantages.

Nostalgia
Eliot was writing in a period of perceived rapid change – something which people tend to find discomforting – as we know to our cost in the modern age. One of the strong elements of appeal, particularly in her early novels, was the picture she drew there of a settled, cohesive village life. Contemporary readers revelled in the nostalgia of it all; even at this distance of time there is still an element of this appeal for a modern reader.

Personal memories
Setting the action of her novels in the relatively recent past allowed Eliot to use memories of her own childhood. This was particularly true

of *The Mill on the Floss*. U. C. Knoepflmacher, in his *Laughter and Despair: Readings in Ten Novels of the Victorian Era* (University of California Press, 1971) has pointed out that even the dates in this novel tally, Eliot and Maggie both being born in 1819, whereas both Isaac Evans and Tom were born in 1816.

A safe perspective

From the safe perspective of her position several decades on, Eliot could both emphasize the continuity of the past with her present and imply reassuringly that events which seemed to threaten crisis at the time turned out, in fact, to be a storm in a teacup. For instance, the local passions which led 'six or seven men in smock-frocks with hay-forks in their hands' to threaten the railway agents who arrive in the Middlemarch area must have seemed absurd by the time the novel was published: the coming of the railway had not been, in fact, the disaster once anticipated by countryside dwellers.

Six or seven men in smock-frocks ...

NARRATIVE APPROACH

We are all used to reading novels in which the narrator is **omniscient**, yet since modern novelists are not in the habit of both telling the story and simultaneously intruding into it, Eliot's style can take some getting used to.

It is true that in her earlier novels, Eliot's intrusions were not always successful by modern standards – or even sometimes by contemporary ones (see Contemporary criticism p. 62–3). Very occasionally, in these early novels, she appears coyly intrusive: when introducing us to Hall Farm in *Adam Bede* she invites us to 'put your face to one of the panes in the right-hand window: what do you see?' But in her later novels, Eliot is far more sophisticated, presenting in *Middlemarch* a confident, authoritative narrative voice which conveys both ironical humour and sympathetic understanding. A good example of this can be found in Chapter 15 where Eliot straightforwardly introduces Lydgate from the point of view of someone far better acquainted with him than the other fictional characters:

> At present I have to make the new settler Lydgate better known to any one interested in him than he could possibly be even to those who had seen the most of him since his arrival in Middlemarch.

Eliot goes on to give us a wealth of information about him, including the sly: 'he cared not only for "cases", but for John and Elizabeth, especially Elizabeth'. For further discussion of narrative voice see Major works p 47–50.

PLOTS

The incomer/misfit

Strangers often provide a stimulus to events in Eliot's novels. In *Adam Bede* the narrator, Captain Townley (his name suggests the limited perspective which a 'townie' might present in such a rural area), is an intruder. But Hetty and Dinah are also incomers. In *The Mill on the Floss,* the Tullivers are an old established family but Maggie, that 'small mistake of nature', is the cuckoo in the nest who is from infancy unable or unwilling to conform. The stranger in *Silas Marner* is, of course, the **eponymous** hero.

Interrelatedness

The plotting of Eliot's novels is seldom straightforward. Even a relatively short and simple novel like *Silas Marner* has three areas of interest: Silas, the rural inhabitants of Raveloe, and the Casses. A multi-plot novel like *Middlemarch* presents us with a galaxy of characters and foci of interest.

Eliot's way of dealing with this may superficially remind a modern reader of a television soap. Several chapters concentrate the audience on one focus of interest before we are switched to another. However, Eliot's method is rather more complex and repays study. Just as Shakespeare often gives us a sub-plot which echoes the main one thematically, the whole being linked through **metaphorical language**, so Eliot subtly interrelates characters and ideas in her novels. For Eliot each person exists in 'the same embroiled medium, the same troublous fitfully-illuminated life' (*Middlemarch*, Ch. 30).

> ## KEYWORDS
>
> An eponymous protagonist, from the Greek, 'giving his name to', is one who gives his or her name to the title of the work. Other examples from Eliot are *Adam Bede* and *Daniel Deronda*.
>
> Metaphorical language employs a figure of speech in which one thing is described in terms of another. For instance, in *Adam Bede*, Hetty's feelings of abandonment and isolation on her lover's departure are conveyed thus: 'She was all alone on her little island of dreams, and all around her was the dark unknown water where Arthur was gone.'

We are reminded of this through deliberate parallels of character and event; some of which are signalled by the names of the discrete books of *Middlemarch*: 'Waiting for Death', 'Two Temptations', 'Three Love Problems'. It will help to be on the look-out for both the illuminating parallels and the metaphorical language that knits them together as you read. Remember that a Victorian would, in all likelihood, have had a great deal more available time to read than you – and if they were reading a novel like *Middlemarch*, which appeared in serialized parts, would probably read and re-read it several times before the appearance of the next instalment. Eliot assumed this slow, considered reading style in her audience – and it is one which pays dividends.

✳ ✳ ✳*SUMMARY* ✳ ✳ ✳

Eliot's novels tend to:

- have rural settings;

- be located 40–60 years in the past;

- involve a misfit/incomer;

- have complex plots, which are linked by parallels of character, by theme and by metaphorical language.

Major Themes 5

Eliot's concerns are broadly social: her interest focuses on the personal and the effects on the individual. From *Adam Bede* through *The Mill on the Floss*, *Silas Marner*, *Middlemarch* and *Daniel Deronda* she develops ideas about the family. One important theme that runs through her novels is the conflict between altruism and egoism. Other central themes are the part played by self-deception, misunderstanding and deception; the power of speculation and gossip, and the balance of power in relationships.

ALTRUISM V. EGOISM

Selfish desires are something to be fought against and conquered in Eliot's novels: 'I know no speck as troublesome as self' the narrator declares in *Middlemarch* (Ch. 42). Her novels present some characters who are unable to move out of self-absorption and others who learn painful lessons as a result of trying to struggle towards a less egocentric world view. Barbara Hardy, in *The Novels of George Eliot* (Athlone Press, 1959), sees the characters as being 'sheep or goats' in this respect, and part of a complex pattern within the novels. This patterning highlights themes for the reader and gives shape to the novels: 'the two formal features which are most conspicuous are antithesis, or contrast, on the one hand, and correspondence, or resemblance, on the other'. As readers we are invited to see this pattern in many ways, and whereas in earlier novels the correspondence between characters may be fairly obvious and straightforward (Hetty versus Dinah in *Adam Bede*), this becomes more complex and sophisticated later. Thus in *Middlemarch* there are fruitful parallels between Dorothea and Lydgate – but also between Dorothea and both Rosamond and Celia.

Tragic tension arises in Eliot's novels when characters have to decide whether to focus on their own interests or those of others. We will look at some examples below, first examining two self-indulgent young men (Godfrey Cass from *Silas Marner* and Fred Vincy from *Middlemarch*), then two passionate – and very different – young women (Maggie Tulliver from *The Mill on the Floss* and Gwendolen Harleth from *Daniel Deronda*).

Godfrey Cass

Like Arthur Donnithorne in *Adam Bede*, Godfrey is the local young squire, prone to 'natural irresolution and moral cowardice'. His affair with Molly occurred prior to the opening of *Silas Marner*, but his well-meaning decision to cope with 'his own vicious folly' by secretly marrying her has resulted in the 'blight on his life', which clouds his existence at the opening of the novel. 'For four years he had thought of Nancy Lammeter, and wooed her with tacit patient worship' – but he is unable to propose. He is trapped between his desire for Nancy, his need to provide sufficiently well for his wife so as to avoid her searching him out, the disapproval of his father, and blackmail from an unpleasant younger brother. Again like Arthur, he deals with his problems by attempting to drown them in drink. His lack of resolution is such that he vaguely hopes for some deliverance by miracle; he falls back on 'the old disposition to rely on chances which might be favourable to him and save him from betrayal'.

When the miracle occurs – his wife is found dead and his natural daughter claimed by Silas Marner – Godfrey is only too happy to seize this serendipitous opportunity. But his abandonment of his moral responsibilities catches up with him by the end of the novel. Again, like Arthur, he tries to solve the problem by throwing material things at it – too late. He and Nancy cannot solve their ache of childlessness by attempting to 'buy' his daughter Eppie at this late stage. Godfrey recognizes his mistakes. He says to his wife at the end of the novel: 'It's part of my punishment, Nancy, for my daughter to dislike me ... when I'd shirked doing a father's part too.'

Fred Vincy

Fred Vincy in *Middlemarch*, is a character nearly ruined by natural egoism and a misguided expectation that a future inheritance will protect him from the consequences of his own behaviour. His very first appearance in the novel, in Chapter 11, has him disregarding anyone else's convenience but his own: 'the family laggard' comes down extremely late for breakfast and is disparaging about the proffered 'coffee and buttered toast', arrogantly demanding that a freshly cooked meal be provided for him alone. His natural selfishness means that he fails to understand others – Eliot provides this barbed comment in relation to him: 'The difficult task of knowing another soul is not for young gentlemen whose consciousness is chiefly made up of their own wishes.'

When Fred asks Caleb Garth to guarantee a loan for a substantial sum, it is with the optimistic intention that he will raise the money himself quite easily. When in the event he cannot, Fred's first feeling of disquiet comes from the personal: 'he must seem dishonourable, and sink in the opinion of the Garths'- an inconvenience when he wishes to appear favourably before them in the guise of suitor to their daughter, Mary. It is not until he hears Mr and Mrs Garth discuss how they as a family can cope with their new financial difficulty, that Fred recognizes that this debacle is going to affect other people, not just himself: 'He had not occupied himself with the inconvenience and possible injury that his breach might occasion them, for this exercise of the imagination on other people's needs is not common with hopeful young gentlemen.'

In the event, Fred is saved by the fact of not getting his expected inheritance, by continuing help from Caleb Garth, supported by his own endeavours, and by the love of Mary.

Passionate young women – Maggie Tulliver

In the section of *The Mill on the Floss* entitled 'The Great Temptation', Eliot presents us with a very difficult moral dilemma: Maggie must chose between her love for Stephen Guest, and her sense of duty to her cousin Lucy Deane and to her admirer Philip Wakem. On the one

Philip Wakem

Lucy Deane

LOVE

DUTY

Stephen Guest

Maggie Tulliver

The great temptation.

hand, Eliot creates a compelling sense of the powerful, almost overwhelming mutual attraction that Maggie and Stephen have for each other. We are told that it is like 'opium'; that their feeling has 'the solemnity belonging to all deep human passion'; that he 'loves with his whole soul.' Stephen puts forward the most cogent arguments for his breaking his engagement to Maggie's cousin, Lucy – although these might be perceived as more reasonable by a contemporary reader than in Eliot's own day. He tries to persuade Maggie that their mutual love 'is natural' and by the discovery of it they 'have been saved from a mistake'. He points out that a mere 'outward faithfulness' to their previous lovers would be nothing but a sham – and a sham for which they would not, eventually, be grateful: 'there may be misery in it for them as well as for us'. Moreover, the reader is acutely aware, during these tender scenes, that this represents a glorious opportunity for Maggie, one chance of real joy in an otherwise dourly bleak life.

On the other hand, Maggie's own judgement, and, it would appear, Eliot's, are unflinchingly on the side of renunciation. Maggie tells Stephen: 'Many things are difficult and dark to me; but one thing I see quite clearly – that I must not, cannot seek my own happiness by sacrificing others.' Once Maggie has temporarily abandoned her principled position by allowing herself to drift off with Stephen in the boat, she is severe in judgement on herself: 'The irrevocable wrong that must blot her life had been committed: she had brought sorrow into the lives of others – into the lives that were knit up with hers by trust and love.' She is absolutely right but she suffers acutely for her mistake afterwards.

Gwendolen Harleth

Daniel Deronda provides us with the fascinating Gwendolen Harleth. In Chapter 4, the narrator, with delicately judged irony informs us:

> Always she was the princess in exile, who in the time of famine was to have her breakfast-roll made of the finest-bolted flour from the seven thin ears of wheat, and in a general decampment was to have her silver fork kept out of the baggage.

The narrator goes on to pose the rhetorical question of why this should be so before providing us with the answer: people like this share 'a strong determination to have what was pleasant, with a total fearlessness in making themselves disagreeable or dangerous when they did not get it'. Gwendolen's self-absorption allows herself to glide over early difficulties with more ease than most; even by the end of the novel she still has 'the implicit impression which had accompanied her from childhood, that whatever surrounded her was somehow specially for her'. This impression is so strong that she fails to understand until the last possible moment that Daniel Deronda, the man who she idolizes, is in fact going to marry someone else. Up to this point, Gwendolen has not really considered the lives of others except in so far as they have affected her personally: the revelation of Daniel's quite separate agenda comes as something of a shock.

KNOWING YOURSELF AND OTHERS
This is another central theme; moreover it is inextricably linked to Eliot's preoccupation with altruism and egoism. Daniel Cottom points out in his *Social Figures: George Eliot, Social History and Literary Representation* (University of Minnesota Press, 1987):

> It is the presumption of self-discovery through self-sacrifice that constitutes the running argument of all of Eliot's writing.

Seeing what you want to see – *Adam Bede*
Adam Bede provides good examples of people seeing what they want to see rather than reality. Hetty sees Arthur, and Adam sees Hetty exclusively as 'answers to [their] own yearnings'. Thus Adam persists in 'attributing imaginary virtues' to Hetty: 'he created the mind he believed in out of his own, which was large, unselfish, tender', despite all evidence to the contrary. His determined ability to believe in his own subjective fantasy of Hetty is illustrated particularly well by the incident in which he realizes that Hetty is the owner of a rather expensive locket which contains two locks of hair: Hetty's and some hair of a much lighter colour. Initially, he correctly fears the worst: 'There was something in Hetty's life unknown to him; that while he had been rocking himself in the hope that she would come to love him, she was already loving another.' However, even in the face of such concrete evidence, Adam's mind goes on to weave 'for himself an ingenious web of probabilities' in this situation. He decides that because she is so 'fond of finery' she has bought it herself. He has problems with her obvious discomfort at his seeing the locket, but explains this away to his own complete satisfaction by her acceptance that 'it was wrong for her to spend her money on it, and she knew that Adam disapproved of finery'. This, moreover, is 'a proof she cared about what he liked and disliked'. He decides that the locket must contain 'a bit of her father's or mother's [hair], who had died when she was a child, and she would naturally put a bit of her own along with it'. He moves himself from anxious suspicion to complacent self-satisfaction in no time at all.

Self-deception in *Middlemarch* – Dorothea and Lydgate

Middlemarch also provides many examples of self-deception and because of the way in which the narrator moves from a particular example to generalization, we are all invited to see ourselves as part of 'the fellowship of illusion', interpreting things with our own 'creative inclination'. Lovers are particularly prone to self-delusion: Eliot refers to the 'few imaginative weeks called courtship' in this novel – this is a recurrent idea in her writing. Gwendolen, in *Daniel Deronda* is 'walking amid delusions' on her wedding day and Maggie feels that she and Stephen are enveloped in an 'enchanted haze' whilst they are on the river in *The Mill on the Floss*.

Despite the fact that her sister Celia points out to Dorothea her error with regard to Sir James Chettam and says: 'You always see what nobody else sees; it is impossible to satisfy you; yet you never see what is quite plain,' Dorothea goes on to perceive Casaubon, too, in her own self-created image. Thus when she looks into his mind she sees 'reflected there in vague labyrinthine extension every quality she herself had brought'.

Lydgate does exactly the same. Despite his experience with Laure, Lydgate repeats his previous error and constructs Rosamond as he wants her to be, rather than what she is. His suppositions are entirely rose-tinted, something which is betrayed by the language used when he sees Rosamond as 'a creature who would bring him the sweet furtherance of satisfying affection – beauty – repose – such help as our thoughts get from the summer sky and the flower-fringed meadows'. Lydgate extends his optimism to encompass the behaviour of his future father-in-law, who he imagines will provide a useful sum 'in the form of a dowry, to make payment easy'.

Eliot tells us in this novel that 'we are all born in moral stupidity'. As Suzanne Bailey has pointed out in her paper 'Reading the "Key": George Eliot and the higher criticism' (*Women's Writing*, Vol. 3, No. 2, 1996):

> Both Dorothea and Lydgate 'emerge from that stupidity' when they take responsibility for their partner, not as an idealized object, but as a being with their own 'centre of self.'

This involves both in suffering and a voyage of self-discovery, which runs alongside the discoveries that they make about others.

Self-deception where love is not involved

The above examples have concerned the self-deception of those in love. In *Middlemarch*, Bulstrode is a good example of someone who, through 'the use of wide phrases for narrow motives' has managed to conceal from himself and others the sheer hypocrisy of his behaviour. The narrator points out to us, though, that he is not a hypocrite who has consciously set out to deceive from the start:

> He was simply a man whose desires had been stronger than his theoretic beliefs, and who had gradually explained the gratification of his desires into satisfactory agreement with those beliefs. (Chapter 61)

Typically, this behaviour is then generalized with the thought 'if this is hypocrisy, it is a process which shows itself occasionally in all of us.'

In *Daniel Deronda* there are several examples of self-deception. One which does not involve a couple is the Arrowpoints' attitude towards their daughter. Although Catherine's 'persistence in declining suitable offers' of marriage has alarmed her parents, they do not suspect for one moment that she might be nurturing a passion for her music teacher. The narrator points out that 'the truth is something different from the habitual lazy combinations begotten by our wishes'. We are reminded of the earlier remark that 'all meanings, we know, depend on the key of interpretation'.

MISUNDERSTANDING AND DECEPTION

Misunderstanding often arises because of self-deception in Eliot's novels, however, it also occurs quite naturally. For instance, Ladislaw's assumption that after Casaubon's death, Dorothea has been left 'a rich widow' means that he is far too proud to admit his true feelings for her when he is leaving the town lest he be branded a cheap fortune-hunter. He has no idea what the actual terms of Casaubon's will were.

When Godfrey finally nerves himself to tell Nancy the truth about his relationship to Eppie in Chapter 18 of *Silas Marner*, he does not get the reaction he expects – no anger, only deep regret. She says:

> Godfrey, if you had but told me this six years ago, we could have done our duty by the child. Do you think I'd have refused to take her in, if I'd known she was yours?

This is a terrible moment of realization: 'Godfrey felt all the bitterness of an error that was not simply futile, but had defeated its own end.'

Eliot's novels are redolent with deliberate deception and this often provides a cornerstone of the plot. For instance, in *Silas Marner*, William Dane's early and cruel deception of his best friend causes Silas to leave Lantern Yard and journey out blindly to Raveloe. Then Godfrey's wish to keep his first marriage a secret both generates Dunsey's behaviour and allows Silas to bring up Eppie as his own.

In *Adam Bede* it is Arthur's careful efforts to conceal his dalliance with Hetty, despite his 'open-looking and candid' appearance, which cause events to move as they do. Then Hetty's desperate attempt to conceal her pregnancy leads to her own downfall and changed lives in Hayslope.

THE POWER OF GOSSIP

Gossip is a power of considerable influence in Eliot's novels. In *The Mill on the Floss*, the narrator tells us that 'public opinion is always of the feminine gender' – and it is certainly true that 'the fabric of opinion' in *Middlemarch* is woven principally by women: Mrs Plymdale, Mrs Bulstrode, Mrs Vincy, Mrs Cadwaller, Mrs Dollop, Mrs Hackbutt and Mrs Taft being amongst those responsible.

These women relish gossip, feed on it and spread it – but the men enjoy it too. When the scandal erupts over Bulstrode and Lydgate in Chapter 71, the news spread fast, 'gathering round it conjectures and comments which gave it new body and impetus' and giving rise to an increased number of social gatherings:

> The business was felt to be so public and important that it required dinners to feed it, and many invitations were just then issued and accepted on the strength of this scandal ... wives, widows and single ladies took their work and went out to tea oftener than usual; and all public conviviality, from the Green Dragon to Dollop's, gathered a zest which could not be won from the question whether the Lords would throw out the Reform Bill.

The tone of the gossip takes on a hysterical note: Mrs Hackbutt gives it as her opinion that Mrs Bulstrode 'ought to separate from' her husband and exclaims, 'Fancy living with such a man! I should expect to be poisoned.'

It is tremendously important to the small-minded that no one steps out of line. The narrator remarks ironically early in *Middlemarch* that 'sane people did what their neighbours did, so that if any lunatics were at large, one might know and avoid them'. In *The Mill on the Floss*, Dr Kenn is horrified by the powerful, irrational and hypocritical attitudes rigidly presented in the face of Maggie's return to St Ogg's after her debacle with Stephen. All his well-meaning efforts 'to open the ears of women to reason, and their conscience to justice' fail. The power of popular opinion can be overwhelmingly strong: in *Adam Bede*, Hetty's shame at her transgression and her awareness of the social consequences outweigh her feelings of love and pity for her baby.

Small-minded prejudice

Small-minded prejudice routinely comes into operation in Eliot's work with someone who is in any way different from the norm. Thus Maggie in *The Mill on the Floss*, has a difficult childhood because her keen intelligence and unfeminine appearance brand her as a 'small mistake of nature' who does not conform to expectations. Mrs Garth, in *Middlemarch*, 'never poured any pathetic confidences into the ears of her feminine neighbours concerning Mr Garth's want of prudence and the sums he might have had if he had been like other men'. Because of this aberrant behaviour, Mrs Garth is branded by her 'fair neighbours' as 'either proud or eccentric'.

Ladislaw, in *Middlemarch* is an object of suspicion because of his facility with words. Mr Keck thinks that his suspicious foreign background partly accounts for this:

> Ladislaw, if the truth be known, was not only a Polish emissary, but crack-brained, which accounted for the preternatural quickness and glibness of his speech when he got on to a platform – as he did whenever he had the opportunity, speaking with a facility which cast reflections on solid Englishmen generally. (Chapter 46)

In *Silas Marner*, Silas's intelligence works against him too:

> All cleverness, whether in the rapid use of that difficult instrument the tongue, or in some other art unfamiliar to villagers, was in itself suspicious. (Chapter 1)

As with Ladislaw, his exceptional abilities, shown when Marner gives 'stuff' to Sally Oates which cures her, are accounted for by his 'foreign' background: 'now it was all clear how he should have come from unknown parts, and be so 'comical-looking''. The fact that he is afflicted by fits underlines Marner's 'difference'.

The ability to provide 'stuff' of a healing nature mean that the Irwine sisters in *Adam Bede* are regarded with similar awe. They must be 'deep in the science of medicine' and this, together with their unfortunate looks makes them an object of suspicion. Like Marner, they are used to frighten children:

> They were used with great effect as a means of taming refractory children, so that at the sight of poor Miss Anne's sallow face, several small urchins had the terrified sense that she was cognizant of all their worst misdemeanours, and knew the precise number of stones with which they intended to hit Farmer Britton's ducks. (Chapter 5)

Silas Marner shows clearly the superstition, born of ignorance, which flourished amongst the ill-educated poor. When Marner's money is stolen, another 'foreigner', the pedlar, is blamed and public opinion gallops away with this idea into gratuitous elaboration and an absurd course of action:

> By way of throwing further light on this clue of the tinder-box, a collection was made of all the articles purchased from the pedlar at various houses, and carried to the Rainbow to be exhibited there. (Chapter 8)

THE BALANCE OF POWER IN RELATIONSHIPS

Gwendolen and Grandcourt

The portrait of Gwendolen and Grandcourt in *Daniel Deronda* is probably Eliot's subtlest picture of the balance of power in a relationship. Before marriage, Gwendolen fantasises about how she will 'manage him thoroughly' after marriage – this is 'a man over whom she was going to have indefinite power'. She imagines that a part of her management will include ensuring that Grandcourt behaves well towards his ex-mistress; she complacently regards herself as a Lady Bountiful in this respect. At this stage, Grandcourt is quite happy to let her play 'at reigning'.

However, once married, Gwendolen's illusions do not persist for long. She is miserable and her 'belief in her own power of dominating – was utterly gone':

> Already, in seven short weeks, which seemed half her life, her husband had gained a mastery which she could no more resist than she could have resisted the benumbing effects from the touch of a torpedo. Gwendolen's will had seemed imperious in its small girlish sway; but … She had found a will like that of a crab or a boa-constrictor which goes on pinching and crushing without alarm at thunder. (Chapter 35)

Rosamond and Lydgate

Before his marriage, Lydgate sees Rosamond as:

> An accomplished creature who venerated his high musings and
> momentous labours and would never interfere with them; who would
> create order in the home and accounts with still magic, yet keep her
> fingers ready to touch the lute and transform life into romance at any
> moment; who was instructed to the true womanly limit and not a
> hair's-breadth beyond – docile, therefore, and ready to carry out
> behests which came from beyond that limit. (Chapter 36)

The irony of this becomes quite painful once the young couple are
settled into married life. Like Gwendolen, Rosamond has known
'nothing but indulgence', but she is a harder nut to crack. She is
characterized by a 'quiet elusive obstinacy' which, prior to their
marriage, Lydgate insisted on misreading. Thus in Chapter 36, when
she declares, with reference to her engagement, that 'I never give up
anything that I choose to do', Lydgate reads this as 'adorable' 'constancy
of purpose'.

Lydgate finds, to his great sadness, that 'affection did not make her
compliant'. Surprised at 'the terrible tenacity of this mild creature',
Lydgate slowly senses 'an amazed sense of his powerlessness over
Rosamond'.

Although to Lydgate 'his marriage seemed an unmitigated calamity', he
is clear-sighted enough to see the pitfalls ahead. Moreover, it is equally
clear to him that Rosamond will make no effort whatsoever to avoid
them. Therefore, if he is to avoid sinking into 'the hideous fettering of
domestic hate', he will have to take action. It is a sad ending for Lydgate
– but this is a situation which he chose to be in and we can respect him
for taking full responsibility in it:

> Lydgate had accepted his narrowed lot with sad resignation. He had
> chosen this fragile creature, and had taken the burthen of her life upon
> his arms. He must walk as he could, carrying that burthen pitifully.
> (Chapter 81)

The power of a good woman in a relationship

Middlemarch provides several examples of good, strong women who are the making of their man and of the relationship that they are in. These are Mary Garth (in relation to Fred Vincy), and Mrs Garth and Mrs Bulstrode (their husbands). Mary Garth sees clear-sightedly that 'people were so ridiculous with their illusions, carrying their fools' caps unawares, thinking their own lies opaque while everybody else's were transparent' (Chapter 33). She is careful to entertain no illusions about Fred and gives him both wise advice and a direction in life.

Mrs Garth's eminently sensible way of dealing with her husband's deficiencies is to enjoy them, as far as she can, as being an integral part of the person she loves:

> Adoring her husband's virtues, she had early made up her mind to his incapacity of minding his interests, and had met the consequences cheerfully. (Chapter 24)

When Fred confesses to losing the money he had borrowed from her husband, money which was destined for their son's apprenticeship and which Mrs Garth had herself painfully 'scraped together', she applies herself practically to the problem without 'bitter remarks or explosions'.

Perhaps the most touching portrait is that of Mrs Bulstrode. Despite clear evidence of public opinion ranked solidly against her husband when his past misdeeds come to light, her 'loyal spirit' means she has no real hesitation in sticking by him, despite the costs to herself. The scene of their sitting side by side, both crying, is incredibly poignant.

✳ ✳ ✳ *SUMMARY* ✳ ✳ ✳

Eliot's themes include:

- altruism versus egoism;

- self-deception, its consequent misunderstandings, and deception;

- the power of gossip;

- the balance of power in relationships.

Major Works

In this chapter we will look at four different aspects of Eliot's writing: **realism**, characterization, narrative viewpoint, and imagery and word-patterning in relation to her most widely read novels: *Silas Marner, The Mill on the Floss, Adam Bede, Middlemarch* and *Daniel Deronda*.

REALISM

Accuracy of detail

> **KEYWORD**
>
> The word **realism** is much used in literary criticism: it is a somewhat elastic term. It is probably most helpful to think of it meaning life as lived by recognizably ordinary people – and the complete opposite of the unreal or fantastic.

Eliot was the most painstakingly conscientious researcher. Before embarking on *Adam Bede*, she made notes on Fairholt's *Costume in England* to ensure that every nuance of Hetty's fashionable aspirations were correct. She also read assiduously all the issues of the *Gentleman's Magazine* for the period covered by the novel so that she would be certain that any minutiae about weather or flora and fauna could be accurate. This, together with a sharp eye for the particular, gives us carefully observed passages such as the early pages of *Adam Bede* where the narrator is arriving on the outskirts of Hayslope in springtime:

> And directly below them the eye rested on a more advanced line of hanging woods … still showing the warm tints of the young oak and the tender green of the ash and lime … He saw (in the foreground) … the level sunlight lying like transparent gold among the gently-curving stems of the feathered grass and the tall red sorrel, and the white umbels of the hemlocks lining the busy hedgerows. (Chapter 2)

The same acuity, combined with wry humour, gives us both vivid locations, characterized by a wealth of interior domestic detail, and delightful cameos throughout the novels. Eliot is particularly successful when describing the behaviour and language of small children – like Totty in *Adam Bede*, engaged here in copying her mother:

'Mummy, my iron's twite told; pease put it down to warm.' The small chirruping voice that uttered this request came from a sunny-haired girl between three and four, who, seated on a high chair at the end of the ironing table, was arduously clutching the handle of a miniature iron with her tiny fat fist, and ironing rags with an assiduity that required her to put her little red tongue out as far as anatomy would allow. (Chapter 6)

Eliot is equally accurate when describing animals. There are so many examples – perhaps one of the best being the encounter in Chapter 39 between the two dogs Monk and Fag when Mr Brooke visits his tenant Dagley in *Middlemarch*. Fag, the resident sheepdog, is considering taking up an aggressive stance when Brooke enters the yard, but thinks better of it and opts for assumed nonchalance when Brooke's dog follows him in: 'Seeing Monk enter the yard after some outside loitering, Fag seated himself again in an attitude of observation.' Feeling foolish as a consequence, Fag sulks and follows his master, 'sullenly evading some small and probably charitable advances on the part of Monk'.

It is this carefully grounded descriptive detail that makes Eliot's fictional world so solidly and incontestably 'real' for the reader. The narrator in *Adam Bede* declares that 'my strongest effort is ... to give a faithful account of men and things as they have mirrored themselves in my mind' (Ch. 17) – and there is every reason to suppose that this was also Eliot's ambition. Perhaps we should view this with some caution though: Caroline Levine, in her essay 'Women or Boys? Gender, Realism, and the Gaze in *Adam Bede*' (*Women's Writing*, Vol. 3 No. 2, 1996) points out that Eliot follows this remark by saying that the mirror is 'doubtless defective'. Levine goes on:

> This is indeed a curious realism, relying as it does on the mind of the subject, and refusing to promise either clarity or accuracy.

Valued by contemporaries

Eliot's novels were particularly valued by contemporary readers because of their vivid depiction of a vanishing way of life. Just as many early addicts of *The Archers* in recent times believed that those characters and places were real, so many contemporaries thought that Eliot's novels presented documentary evidence of people and locations that the author had known. This aspect of Eliot's work was underscored by Cross's biography of her: the carefully sanitized version presented Eliot as a guardian of the recent historical past and of traditional moral values.

And by modern critics

Modern critics have drawn attention to Eliot's success as a realist writer. J. Hillis Miller, in his essay entitled 'Optic and Semiotic in *Middlemarch*', included in *George Eliot*, edited by Harold Bloom (Chelsea House, 1986), contrasts Eliot's technique with the more emblematic quality of Dickens' writing. He admires the 'fullness of characterization and the accompanying circumstantiality of social detail in *Middlemarch*' and points out that 'they make this novel perhaps the masterwork of Victorian realism'. Similarly, Alexander Welsh, in an essay included in *The Cambridge Guide to George Eliot* edited by George Levine (CUP 2001) talks of the 'Wordsworthian sense of place [which] gives the countryside a felt pastness' in *The Mill on the Floss.*

Ian Adam, in his essay 'The Structural Realisms in *Adam Bede*', printed in *Nineteenth Century Fiction* (September 1975) differentiates between various kinds of realism which 'have broad structural significance' in that novel. He gives examples of pictorial, analytic and dramatic realism before going on to examine the abundant and leisurely visual detail of the novel, pointing out that the frequent emphasis on objects perceived visually, as opposed to by any of the other senses, helps to give solidity to Eliot's world. He goes on to make the observation that the choice of the definite rather than the indefinite article in passages of description enhances this effect. He also observes that even in this early novel the 'abundance of local incident and anecdote' makes the inhabitants of Loamshire leap into life and gives us the sense that any one of the most minor characters could well be a major player in a story of their own. Other critics have admired Eliot's use of technical terms where necessary and the convincing way in which she intermingles her fiction with actual events and real people – like mention of Burke and Hare, the body snatchers, in *Middlemarch.*

'The classic realist text' debate

Later in the 1970s intensive academic debate arose about 'the classic realist text', as it came to be called, and its inadequacies. *Middlemarch*, as the epitome of the genre, tended to feature largely in the discussion. An important voice here was Colin MacCabe, in *James Joyce and the Revolution of the Word*, (Palgrave, 1979), who contrasted what he saw as Joyce's liberated use of language with the altogether inferior example of 'the classic realist text' as exemplified by *Middlemarch.* Catherine Belsey, in her *Critical Practice* (Routledge, 1980), developed this line of argument and popularized it.

In recent years more of a balance has been achieved. David Lodge, in his seminal essay '*Middlemarch* and the Idea of the Classic Realist Text', revised by the author for inclusion in *New Casebooks: Middlemarch* (Macmillan Press, 1992), demonstrates that McCabe might have assumed that Eliot's style was rather less complex and successful than in fact it is. Other more recent critics have recognized the actual complexity and degree of innovation behind what was assumed by some to be a simple illusionist technique and mere conservatism. For a fuller discussion of these modern critical attitudes, see the chapter on Modern criticism.

CHARACTERIZATION

Most readers would agree that Eliot peoples her novels with a range of unforgettable characters. Whilst it is true that Dunsey Cass in *Silas Marner* is something of a standard villainous stereotype, he is nonetheless a minor character. Grandcourt, in *Daniel Deronda*, is another unchanging, unrepentant and powerful villain; however, this more major player is drawn with fascinating subtlety. He is reminiscent of a snake, with his passions 'of the intermittent, flickering kind' (Ch. 15), his indolent demeanour and his highly intelligent manoeuvring. In the same novel, Gwendolen is a masterly and convincing portrait of contradictions: this is a girl who flirts and displays herself as sexually attractive whilst being repelled by sexual contact, who appears supremely self-confident and in control but who still needs to creep insecurely into her mother's bed for reassurance. Perhaps a measure of Eliot's success in her writing is that she creates characters who can surprise us whilst remaining wholly believable. In *The Mill on the Floss*, the over-critical Aunt Glegg, for instance, is, in the end, one of the few to be supportive of Maggie after her debacle with Stephen.

So how does Eliot manage to create such psychologically convincing and interesting characters? The answer lies in a combination of the way her narrator comments on the characters (although this will largely be dealt with in the next section), the characters' thought processes, their speech, and their actions and interactions with others.

Narrative style

Eliot's style of narration often involves a summary introduction to a character, typically a few terse, often barbed, comments, the truth of which we later discern for ourselves when we see that person in action. For instance, in *Middlemarch*, we meet Mr Brooke in the second, fairly short, paragraph of Chapter 1. We are told he is 'a man nearly sixty, of acquiescent temper, miscellaneous opinions, and uncertain vote'. The truth of these phrases will be evidenced in no time at all as the novel proceeds. Eliot then goes on to draw attention to a key aspect of Brooke's personality: his combination of charitable intentions and miserly habits, before moving seamlessly into a generalization naturally provoked by this train of thought:

> For the most glutinously indefinite minds enclose some hard grains of habit; and a man has been seen lax about all his own interests except the retention of his snuff-box, concerning which he was watchful, suspicious, and greedy of clutch.

This is quite typical of Eliot's style: just when we were about to dismiss Brooke as being wholly unlike ourselves, the generalization invites us to consider more widely: we may know others who are very similar – we may even resemble this person.

Convincing thoughts and feelings

Once we have been introduced to a main character, we share their thoughts and feelings. In Chapter 4 of *The Mill on the Floss*, Maggie is enjoying being alone in the mill, thinking about the spiders that she sees covered with a fine powdering of flour:

> She wondered if they had any relations outside the mill, for in that case there must be a painful difficulty in their family intercourse: a fat and floury spider, accustomed to take his fly well dusted with meal, must suffer a little at a cousin's table where the fly was au naturel, and the lady spiders must be mutually shocked at each other's appearance.

This is a convincing representation of a childish train of thought which is wholly appropriate for a little girl in Maggie's circumstances. At this stage in the novel, we, as readers, have not yet encountered Maggie's relations. However, as soon as they enter the novel we understand exactly why this child has been sensitized to consider relationships in this way – with overtones of disapproval, disdain and awkwardness.

The language chosen by Eliot for a character's thoughts is always highly appropriate. In addition, Eliot tends to use **free indirect speech** extensively to produce sophisticated and complex effects. A good example of this is Hetty, the naïve fantasist from *Adam Bede*, here dwelling on a future secret marriage to Arthur Donnithorne. She uses simple vocabulary, apart from the more particular 'brocaded', which reflects her ambitious interest in fashion, repeats 'and' as a connective, and demonstrates very faulty logic:

KEYWORD

Free indirect speech (sometimes the words 'style' or 'discourse' are used rather than 'speech') is when a fictional character's thoughts and ideas are presented in the kind of vocabulary we would expect them to use themselves but are recorded in the third rather than the first person singular. Ironic ambiguity can be created when it is not entirely clear whether the author is at one with, or at an ironic distance from, the fictional creation.

> Captain Donnithorne couldn't like her to go on doing work: he would like to see her in nice clothes, and thin shoes, and white stockings, perhaps with silk clocks to them; for he must love her very much – no one else had ever put his arm around her and kissed her in that way …
> And nothing could be as it had been again: perhaps some day she should be a grand lady, and ride in a coach, and dress for dinner in a brocaded silk, with feathers in her hair, and her dress sweeping the ground. (Chapter 15)

Eliot is particularly good at dramatizing conflict and choice within the mind of a character. Arthur Donnithorne's difficulty over Hetty is presented in two paragraphs of Chapter 12 – in the first of which he feels 'he *must not* see her alone again' whilst in the subsequent one he argues himself round to the more attractive 'he *must* see her again'. Gwendolen Harleth's decision to first refuse, then to accept Grandcourt is also very cleverly done.

Convincing dialogue

Eliot had an excellent ear for dialogue; she seems to have been particularly sensitive to the musicality of voices. This was evident in the cameo of Totty, quoted on page 40. In *Middlemarch* the characters are noticeably differentiated by the tone as well as by the content of what they say. Casaubon speaks with a 'balanced sing-song neatness of [his] speech.' Celia always speaks with 'quiet, staccato evenness' whilst her sister Dorothea has a 'musical intonation which in moments of deep but quiet feeling made her speech like a fine bit of recitative'. Mrs Cadwaller has 'the clearest chiselled utterance', whilst Madame Laure's 'voice was a soft cooing' and Rosamund speaks in a 'silvery, neutral way'. Thus before we even hear the content of what the characters have to say, the very way in which they speak tells us a great deal about their personalities.

There is also a great deal of difference in the language that characters use. Casaubon is characterized by the dead, pedantic precision of his speech, his 'chilling rhetoric', and his pomposity of diction. He 'delivered himself with precision, as if he had been called upon to make a public statement', 'in a measured official tone'. Thus his private conversation is delivered with the meticulous clipped care of a formal speech. This is the complete opposite of Brooke, who manages to make even a public statement sound like casual, rambling conversation.

Blanche Williams, in *George Eliot: A Biography* (Macmillan, 1936) noticed another contrast in *Adam Bede*: 'After the long, mellifluous flow of Dinah's speeches, Mrs Poyser's are like whip-cracks.' Mrs Poyser is one of several characters whose speech is indicated as being that of an uneducated country dweller by use of dialect. Eliot does this very successfully; steering clear of the possible pitfalls in giving characters this mode of speech. She wrote in a letter to W. W. Skeat that her 'inclination to be as clear as I could to the rendering of dialect, both in words and spelling, was constantly checked by the artistic duty of being generally intelligible' (Haight, *Letters* ix, 39).

Convincing actions and interactions

You can pick up any novel by Eliot and find with ease yet another example of a psychologically convincing interaction. Sometimes these do not even involve much in the way of the spoken word. There is, for instance, Mrs Bulstrode's visit to her niece, Rosamund Vincy, in Chapter 31 of *Middlemarch*. 'Rosamund felt sure that her aunt had something particular to say'; nevertheless, conversation does not flow smoothly at the outset because both women are distracted by the attire of the other. Despite her pressing mission to discover whether her niece is, or is not yet, engaged to Lydgate, 'the quilling inside Rosamund's bonnet was so charming that it was impossible not to desire the same kind of thing for Kate, and Mrs Bulstrode's eyes, which were rather fine, rolled round that ample quilled circuit, while she spoke'. Rosamund does not concentrate fully on her aunt's opening remark for a similar reason:

> 'What is that, aunt?' Rosamund's eyes were also roaming over her aunt's large embroidered collar.

NARRATIVE VIEWPOINT

In an essay entitled 'German Wit: Heinrich Heine' (January 1856), Eliot made a significant statement which could stand as her aesthetic manifesto: 'Art is the nearest thing to life: it is a mode of amplifying experience and extending our contact with our fellow-men beyond the bounds of our personal lot.' She amplified this by emphasizing the importance of our being able to feel for 'the peasant in all his coarse apathy, and the artisan in all his suspicious selfishness'.

Eliot achieves this important aim of extending our sympathies through her deft use of the narrative voice in her novels. As readers we are seldom allowed to be complacent, to feel superior to even the most unattractive individuals. On the rare occasions when Eliot withdraws narrative sympathy from characters – Grandcourt in *Daniel Deronda* is a good example – we are conscious of the comparative bleakness of the effect. It will be useful to examine exactly how Eliot manages this, using *Middlemarch* as an example.

Extending our sympathies in *Middlemarch*: Rosamond Vincy

One of Eliot's greatest achievements in *Middlemarch* is to create characters who are at once intolerable and pitiable; Rosamond Vincy is one of these.

Use of irony

Rosamond's behaviour and speech demonstrate clearly to the reader what type of person she is. However, narrative voice is perhaps Eliot's greatest, certainly her subtlest, tool to guide our feelings. From the first, Eliot directs a wicked undercurrent of irony towards Rosamond, insidiously building and escalating this in certain passages. For instance, in Chapter 23 the small detail that Rosamond is 'steered by wary grace and propriety' near the beginning of one paragraph makes one pause for thought. There is, of course, nothing wrong with 'grace and propriety' – but 'wary'? It suggests studied manoeuvring, or at the very least a watchfulness that is worlds away from a young woman's innocent and attractive spontaneity. Next we are told that she cultivates a very particular impression of herself quite purposefully:

> Rosamond never showed any unbecoming knowledge, and was always that combination of correct sentiments, music, dancing, drawing, elegant note-writing, private album for extracted verse, and perfect blond loveliness, which made the irresistible woman for the doomed man of that date.

As we read through Rosamond's thin list of accomplishments, we might begin to question whether these really would encompass perfection in a young lady of the period. (How far would any man, of any era, value 'elegant note-writing' and 'private album for extracted verse' in the love of his life?) Any doubts are banished by the use of the word 'doomed' towards the end. The opening of the next sentence purports to be a plea to look kindly on Rosamond, although as we read on we might guess that the use of four negatives carries the sense of protesting too much. The last part comes with a sting in the tail:

Think no unfair evil of her, pray: she had no wicked plots, nothing sordid or mercenary; in fact, she never thought of money except as something necessary which other people would provide.

Thus our attitude to Rosamond is framed in three sentences.

Straightforward address to the reader

However, Eliot does not allow the reader to dismiss Rosamond; she keeps control of the reader's sympathies. Thus in Chapter 16 when we are, for a while, invited to feel sorry for Lydgate and see him as a potential victim of Rosamond's, Eliot suddenly brings the reader up short:

Poor Lydgate! Or shall I say, Poor Rosamond! Each lived in a world of which the other knew nothing. It had not occurred to Lydgate that he had been a subject of eager meditation to Rosamond, who had neither any reason for throwing her marriage into distant perspective, nor any pathological studies to divert her mind from that ruminating habit, that inward repetition of looks, words, and phrases, which makes a large part of the lives of most girls.

Rosamond reassessed

Then there are the two points in the novel where Rosamond is forced to think about someone else's feelings and wishes. One occurs in Chapter 78, when she who 'had been so little used to imagining other people's states of mind except as material cut into shape by her own wishes' is confronted by the anger and frustration of a man who she had hitherto complacently assumed was in love with her, his sole purpose to ameliorate her boredom by providing opportunities for flirting. Although we are morally behind Ladislaw here, we are made very aware of the effect of his searing directness on Rosamond: 'What another nature felt in opposition to her own was being burnt and bitten into her consciousness.' The alliteration and strength of the verbs impact on the reader; we can't help but feel a degree of sympathy for Rosamond's bewildered suffering. The second occurs in Chapter 81 when Rosamond has an opportunity to act unselfishly – and takes it.

It is one of those surprising, yet convincing, moves by a character so consummately well done by the author. Rosamond chooses to tell Dorothea the truth about Ladislaw's feelings for her, although this damages her own carefully constructed self-image as irresistible to all men. One could argue that in a sense Rosamond is acting selfishly because she is making herself feel better about Ladislaw – but this does not diminish our respect for her. After all, Eliot made it plain to us in the first chapter of this novel that the impulse to feel better about oneself could not be separated, even in the most virtuous, from motives which can lead to good and unselfish actions.

Critical opinion

David Lodge's essay '*Middlemarch* and the Idea of the Classic Realist Text' (op. cit.) refers to and enlarges on an essay by Derek Oldfield in order to consider the complexities of Eliot's narrative voice. He analyzes an early passage describing Dorothea's rather naïve ideas about marriage, analyzing the way in which '**mimesis** and **diegesis** are fused together here'; he points out that this makes considerable demands on the reader. His analysis is well worth reading.

KEYWORDS

Mimesis from the Greek *mime*, to imitate, meaning to represent the truth. A character is behaving or speaking in a way which is convincingly life-like.

Diegesis means a narrative account, in this case by the omniscient narrator.

Critics have found it more difficult to reach a consensus about narrative voice in earlier novels. Dorothea Barrett, in *Vocation and Desire: George Eliot's Heroines* (Routledge, 1989), argues that in *The Mill on the Floss* the 'narrator is chameleon-like, she shifts and changes' while for U. C. Knoepflmacher in *Laughter and Despair: Readings in Ten Novels of the Victorian Era* (University of California Press, 1971), the very same narrator is a 'comical, bookish gentleman.' Perhaps it is more important to look at what the narrator says rather than view him or her as an additional character in the text.

IMAGERY AND WORD-PATTERNING

Telling images

Eliot is a master of the meticulously chosen word and phrase; these are well worth reading carefully for. Sometimes they are put in the mouths of characters, as when, in *Adam Bede*, Adam thinks of Hetty, he likens her to 'a bright-cheeked apple hanging over the orchard wall'. To Adam she appears healthful, seductively inviting – and, given a little effort, just within reach. However, the reader thinks of the Biblical overtones of temptation, forbidden fruit and consequent disaster; moreover of the narrator's earlier warning relating to Hetty, embedded in another fruit image:

> People who love downy peaches are apt not to think of the stone, and sometimes jar their teeth terribly against it. (Chapter 15)

Association

Many critics have commented on the frequent association of Hetty with ideas that are cutely sentimental; this reflects the way in which Adam chooses to regard her. Nina Auerbach in *Woman and the Demon: The Life of a Victorian Myth* (Harvard University Press, 1982) lists similes which include 'kittens, small downy ducks, babies, rose-petals, a young calf' amongst many others. Some associations are more elaborate. For instance, when she is making her way through the woods to meet Arthur in Chapter 12, she gradually comes into our view:

> Ah! there she comes: first a bright patch of colour, like a tropic bird among the boughs, then a tripping figure, with a round hat on and a small basket on her arm, then a deep-blushing, almost frightened, but bright-smiling girl.

Fleetingly (for Hetty herself has responsibility in this affair), we are invited to see her as a Little Red Riding-Hood figure, going as innocent victim into the wolf's clutches.

A character who is given entirely different associations is Casaubon in *Middlemarch*. Paired with Ladislaw, in one of Eliot's deliberate correspondences, he is seen as 'rayless' beside Ladislaw's 'sunny brightness'. Like Grandcourt in *Daniel Deronda* he is associated with the depressing effects of mist and fog: he is described as having 'passionate longings … (which) clung low and mist-like in very shady places'. His efforts at authorship give him 'the sense of moving heavily in a dim and clogging medium'. One of the most memorable passages contrasts Dorothea, newly returned from honeymoon, with her new husband's home:

> Her blooming full-pulsed youth stood there in a moral imprisonment which made itself one with the chill, colourless, narrowed landscape, with the shrunken furniture, the never-read books, and the ghostly stag in a pale fantastic world that seemed to be vanishing from the daylight.
> (Chapter 28)

Here Casaubon is seen by association as emphatically cold, shrivelled and deathly. One can see that Mrs Cadwaller may not have been exaggerating when she earlier described Casaubon as a 'death's head skinned over for the occasion'.

Water imagery

There is no space here to go into Eliot's imagery in detail. One example, water imagery, will have to suffice. The general consensus amongst critics is that Eliot uses water imagery to suggest passions, desires and the ways which an individual might use to expand the meaning of their life. Thus, referring back to Casaubon, Eliot opens Chapter 6 with an ironically flavoured description of that gentleman's decision to 'adorn his life with the graces of female companionship':

> He was determined to abandon himself to the stream of feeling, and perhaps was surprised to find what an exceedingly shallow rill it was.

He was determined to abandon himself to the stream of feeling.

In the early days of courtship, when Dorothea is labouring under her misapprehensions with regard to Casaubon, she thinks: 'His feelings too, his whole experience – what a lake compared to my little pool!' What a hideous contrast with the later experienced reality, commented on as follows:

> Having once embarked on your marital voyage, it is impossible not to be aware that you make no way and that the sea is not within sight – that, in fact, you are exploring an enclosed basin. (Chapter 20)

This imagery is also used in *Silas Marner*. Silas nurses his disappointment and misery in a solitary existence in Raveloe, his 'sap of affection' withering for want of an object. His shrunken life and narrow existence is described in Chapter 2 as being 'like a rivulet that has sunk far down from the grassy fringe of its old breadth into a little shivering thread, that cuts a groove for itself in the barren sand'.

Novels involving rivers, the sea and death by drowning, like *The Mill on the Floss* and *Daniel Deronda* can be seen as a further extension of this idea. Terry Eagleton in his *Criticism and Ideology* (New Left Books,

1976) sees the river in the former novel as a 'symbol of drifting and wayward desire'. Similarly, David Smith, in 'Incest Patterns in Two Victorian Novels', printed in *Literature and Psychology* (summer, 1965) argues that the river in *The Mill on the Floss* is symbolically associated with Maggie's psyche. He suggests that whilst the river at normal flow is associated with Maggie's loss of conscious control, the river at flood represents 'a kind of 'inundation' of her entire being by the forces beneath consciousness'. Gillian Beer, in *Darwin's Plots* (CUP, 2000) makes an interesting observation on the difference between drifting and rowing in Eliot's novels. She points out that whereas drifting seems to suggest 'half-conscious acquiescence in unconscious forces', rowing conveys more 'the activity of the will resisting and attempting to govern such energies'.

Web imagery and other motifs

Eliot's imagery is a subject that has been tackled by many commentators on her work. One of the best introductions is Barbara Hardy's *The Novels of George Eliot: A Study in Form* (Athlone Press, 1959). Gillian Beer (op. cit.) relates scientific language and theory to Eliot's narrative practice and makes useful points about images involving mirrors, windows and reflections. She is also helpful on Eliot's use of web imagery, particularly in *Middlemarch* where the cleverly patterned use of words suggesting webs and woven cloth invites us to see the interrelatedness of people's lives. Elizabeth Weed, concentrating more on *The Mill on the Floss*, contrasts web and water imagery '*The Mill on the Floss* or the Liquidation of Maggie Tulliver', printed in *Genre* (autumn, 1978). Josephine McDonagh examines the use of doors and threshold moments in various novels in her book on Eliot in the 'Writers and their Work' series (Northcote House, 1997).

* * *SUMMARY* * *

- Eliot's realism was achieved by dint of conscientious research. Her success manifests itself in the convincing locations, people and animals in her novels.

- By using narrative control and psychologically accurate thoughts, dialogue and actions for her characters, Eliot is able to create such life-like characters that they can even surprise us.

- Eliot uses narrative techniques to extend our sympathies even to the most repellent characters.

- Imagery is an important structural device in Eliot's novels.

7 Contemporary Criticism

Just as Eliot had herself reviewed many hundreds of books during the period that she was assistant editor of the *Westminster Review,* so her own novels were reviewed on publication in newspapers and various periodicals. These reviews were usually written anonymously. *Scenes of Clerical Life* and *Adam Bede* attracted a certain amount of speculation as to the identity of the author. On the whole, reviewers believed that a male cleric had written *Scenes of Clerical Life;* the contributor to the *Saturday Review* of 29 May 1858 wrote: 'The suspicion is pretty general that George Eliot is an assumed name, screening that of some studious clergyman.' However, opinion divided once *Adam Bede* was published. Thus, the writer dealing with this novel in the *Quarterly Review* of 1 July 1859 suspected that the author might in fact be female because things were 'observed from a woman's point of view' and 'the knowledge of female nature is feminine', whilst the contributor to the *Saturday Review* of 26 February 1859 firmly asserted that 'he is evidently a country clergyman'. Although *The Mill on the Floss* was published in 1860 under the pseudonym, as were all later novels, the actual identity of the author was by then widely known.

Although there were minor criticisms and objections, which will be mentioned below, reviews of Eliot's novels in her lifetime were largely extremely positive.

CHARACTERS

A tremendous achievement

Reviewers were astonished at how well Eliot depicted diverse characters. They recognized the completely convincing truth of these; they were thoroughly entertained by their manners and speech; some were fascinated and delighted to be introduced to people beyond their usual social circles, whilst recognizing that they were probably more entertaining in print than they would be in real life. The critic of *Silas Marner*, writing in *The Times* of 29 April 1861 expressed this latter point memorably. He enjoyed the way that her 'rich vein of humour' combined with 'a peculiar seriousness ... gives inexpressible charm to her descriptions of stupid, poverty-stricken boors'.

There was a real sense of gratitude that Eliot, unlike many contemporary novelists, gave her readers the everyday and the believable – this is expressed by the writer discussing *Scenes of Clerical Life* in the *Saturday Review* of 29 May 1858:

> Considering how unfamiliar most of us are with life in its romantic and adventurous forms, and with men and women of colossal proportion, it is strange that writers rarely have the courage or the talent to depict the characters and experiences which they and we know so well, but fly off at a tangent of improbability as soon as their pens touch paper.

It was with relief that this reviewer encountered a novel that approached its subject matter in a different way. A later contributor to the same publication, writing on *Silas Marner* in a piece which appeared on 13 April 1861, felt that 'the works of George Eliot come on us as a new revelation of what society in quiet English parishes really is and has been'. Once he had read *Adam Bede*, Dickens was particularly taken with the character of Hetty. In an admiring letter to George Eliot, he wrote that he knew 'nothing so skilful, determined and uncompromising' as the picture drawn of her (*The Letters of Charles Dickens*, Vol. 3).

Readers loved the rural characters. A review of *Adam Bede* in *The Times* of 12th April, 1859 is typically enthusiastic:

> All the characters are so true, and so natural, and so racy that we love to hear them talk for the sake of talking. They are so full of strange humours and funny pretty sayings ... The gem of the novel is Mrs Poyser.

Mrs Poyser was universally relished, just as the Dodson family were in the later *The Mill on the Floss*. The reviewer of this novel in *The Times* of 19 May 1860 pointed out that here Eliot:

> takes these characters as we find them in real life – in all their intrinsic littleness. She paints them as she finds them – snapping at each other over the tea-table, eyeing each other enviously at church; privately plotting how to astonish each other by extraordinary display; putting the worst construction on every word and action; officiously proffering advice and predicting calamity; living with perfect content their sordid life of vulgar respectability … The Dodson family will live for ever, and they inspire the work.

The Mill on the Floss was also recognized as breaking new ground in the depiction of children. The writer of the piece published above went on to point out that:

> her description of the childlife is unique. No-one has yet ventured to paint the childlife in all its prosaic reality … . We see all the little squabbling and domineering that goes on among children.

The contributor to the *Spectator* published on 7 April 1860 was also enormously impressed by Eliot's ability to understand and convey 'the child-soul in those things which are common to all children.' He contrasted this with Dickens' 'odd children'. Whilst these were convincing in their own way, Eliot was clearly succeeding in something quite different: 'George Eliot reminds us of what nearly all children are.'

This sense of Eliot's ability to get to the heart of psychological accuracy – the above reviewer went on to say that 'you feel in such a home, a child like Maggie would inevitably grow up into a woman such as Maggie Tulliver is' – was further appreciated in *Middlemarch*. H. Lawrenny, writing in the *Academy* of 1 January 1873 remarked that:

> *Middlemarch* marks an epoch in the history of fiction in so far as its incidents are taken from the inner life … the material circumstances of the outer world are made subordinate and accessory to the artistic

presentation of a definite passage of mental experience, but chiefly as giving a background of perfect realistic truth to a profoundly imaginative psychological study.

Lawrenny pointed out that the promise of this had been present in earlier novels, but the flowering of this ability in *Middlemarch* resulted in characters leaping into life with such extraordinary and unprecedented realism that it verged on the alarming:

> A first perusal of the book seems to have an almost oppressive effect on ordinary readers, somewhat as little children are frightened at a live automaton toy.

For the same reasons, some reviewers appreciated the subtle drawing of Gwendolen and Grandcourt in *Daniel Deronda*. George Saintsbury, writing in the *Academy* of 9 September 1876 admired Eliot's ability to show 'attitudes, transient moods of mind, complex feelings and the like, which is simply unparalleled in any other prose writer'.

Some have reservations

Despite the positive criticism, some reviewers felt that the occasional male character was unconvincing. The contributor to *The National Review* of July 1860 said of Stephen Guest in *The Mill on the Floss* that 'the sketch of him is poor, and does not even realise him strongly to our minds'. A critic of *Silas Marner*, writing in the *Westminster Review* of July 1861, was relieved at the 'masterly' portrait of Godfrey Cass, contrasting this with the 'incompleteness and insufficiency' of both Captain Donnithorne and Stephen Guest. George Saintsbury develops a swingeing criticism of the hero of *Daniel Deronda* in his review for the *Academy* mentioned above, referring to him sarcastically as:

> the blameless young man of faultless feature who clutches his coat-collar continually ... who never does a wicked thing, and never says one that is not priggish – is a person so intolerably dreadful that we not only dislike, but refuse to admit him as possible.

Saintsbury was not the only reviewer who found the hero hopelessly improbable, but he did express it more memorably than most.

Although Eliot's female characters were fairly universally admired, Florence Nightingale, reviewing *Middlemarch* for *Fraser's Magazine* in 1873, was the first in a long line of lady critics to express disappointment at Dorothea's decision to settle for marriage to an 'ardent public man' rather than achieving something on her own account.

The most thoroughgoing criticism of Eliot's characters was made by John Ruskin, in a series of essays that appeared in the magazine *Nineteenth Century* between 1880 and 1881. He compared her very unfavourably with Sir Walter Scott, pointing out that whereas Scott's heroes were people one would wish to emulate, Eliot's were 'flawed', most particularly in *The Mill on the Floss*. He responded with evident distaste to all the characters of this novel, feeling that they were either unpleasant, tiresomely self-absorbed or simply so common and vulgar as to be beneath one's notice.

STYLE

Descriptive power
Readers responded appreciatively to Eliot's ability to convey the English countryside, particularly in her earlier novels. The contributor to the *Bentley's Quarterly Review* of 1 July 1859 said 'we do not know whether our literature anywhere possesses such a closely true picture of purely rural life as *Adam Bede* presents'. Dickens also admired the country setting of this novel; in the letter to Eliot mentioned above, he said that this was 'so real, and so droll and genuine, and yet so selected and polished by art, that I cannot praise it enough'.

For many people, one of Eliot's most notable achievements was the ability she showed, particularly in her earlier novels, to capture and record rural customs, folklore and ways of speech which were, at the time, fast disappearing. Nostalgia for this past way of life made Eliot esteemed simply as a social historian.

Wit and wisdom appreciated

Eliot's wit and wisdom were valued by many. A keen contemporary admirer of her work, Alexander Main, was given permission by the author to extract favourite gems and collect these in his *Wise, Witty and Tender Sayings of George Eliot*. This was a runaway best seller. But she was also taken seriously by academics – something that must have delighted her. James Sully, who established the philosophical journal *Mind* in 1876 for professionals and academics, wrote a piece on 'George Eliot's Art' for an early issue. In this he pointed out that her readers were 'apt to think and speak of her as a discoverer and enforcer of moral truth rather than an artist'.

Eliot's humanity was recognized by the contributor to the *Bentley's Quarterly Review* of 1 July 1859. He appreciated what he called the 'religion of *Adam Bede*' which he perceived as being the need to be tolerant and understanding of others who might at first sight appear to be 'common-place and vulgar'. A critic of *The Mill on the Floss*, writing in *The Times* of 19 May 1860, called it 'a religious novel' not because it contained a great deal in the way of religion but because 'the author is attempting not merely to amuse us as a novelist, but, as a preacher, to make us think and feel'.

A writer reviewing *The Mill on the Floss* in the *Spectator* of 7 April 1860 mentioned the author's 'relish for subdued comedy that constantly brings back to our recollection the best products of Miss Austen's genius'. The reviewer of the first book of *Middlemarch* in the *Spectator* of 16 December 1871 praised 'the great wealth of insight and humour which it contains' whilst the author of a review in the *Nation* of 23 January 1873 had particularly enjoyed the 'irony of situation'. He gave as an example of this the episode where Bulstrode rides home happy, congratulating himself on having got rid of the person who had appeared to threaten his security, only to find that the disgrace which he had tried so hard to avoid is come upon him. The writer linked this with that part of *Adam Bede* where Arthur rides home to take triumphant possession of his estates, only to find that the repercussions of his dalliance with Hetty have caught up with him.

Again, with some reservations

There were mixed feelings about Eliot's moralizing. A contributor to the *Saturday Review* of 7 December 1872, writing on *Middlemarch* conceded that 'as a didactic novel it has scarcely been equalled' but also remarked that 'no talent, no genius itself, can quite overcome the inherent defect of a conspicuous, constantly prominent lesson'. This aspect of Eliot's work had been under fire since the early novels were published. The reviewer of *Adam Bede* in the *Saturday Review* of 26 February 1859 had remarked that there was 'some fault to be found with the manner in which the author intrudes himself in the book'. Another critic of this novel, writing in the *Times* of 12 April 1859, felt that this led to 'want of movement' in the plot. Some felt that since the characters were so excellently brought to life, they would have preferred Eliot to step back more and leave them to speak and act for themselves without quite so much commentary. The author of a review on *Middlemarch* published in the *Nation* of 30 January 1873, thought that although Eliot's 'reflections, if they somewhat injure the movements of the drama, are in themselves so beautiful that we should scarcely care to have them omitted' because they gave the novel 'a peculiar charm'. However, this had a knock-on effect on characterization: it 'greatly damages the whole effect because we see not the men themselves, but the personages as they appear in the author's reflections on them'. This reviewer went on to give Bulstrode as an example, complaining that 'we see a reflection of him, but we never see the man'.

When *Daniel Deronda* was published, several reviewers expressed some sort of objection to Eliot's authorial intrusion quite strongly. George Saintsbury, contributing to the *Academy* of 9 September 1876, said:

> No-one can read *Daniel Deronda* without perceiving and regretting the singular way in which the characters are incessantly pushed back in order that the author may talk about them and about everything in heaven and earth while the action stands still.

Saintsbury, a man of strong personal beliefs, also objected to Eliot's 'proneness to rank certain debateable positions and one-sided points of view among the truths to which it is safe to demand universal assent'.

The contributor to the *Nation* of 19 October 1876 appreciated 'the wit and wisdom' of the novel but thought that 'the chorus is not kept outside the narrative, but delays the action of the piece to press home truths which intelligent readers might in any case discover for themselves'.

Scientific language

On the whole, contemporary reviewers seemed to find Eliot's tendency to scientific language in her later novels pretentious, stilted and unhelpful. The contributor to the *Nation* of 30 January 1873 thought that *Middlemarch* was spoiled by occasional 'scientific conceits'. He quoted the long passage which describes Mrs Cadwaller in Chapter 6 and begins 'Even with a microscope directed on a water-drop', then remarks:

> Now is there in truth one out of a thousand persons who reads this passage who finds that the ten lines of scientific metaphor really make clearer to him the fact, simple enough in itself, that Mrs Cadwaller acted under the influence of a number of infinitely small causes?

Daniel Deronda came in for even more of this kind of criticism. The contributor to the *International Review* of January 1877 remarked tartly that 'dictionaries of science and of positivism ought not to be the necessary vestibule to a book meant for general reading', whilst George Saintsbury, in his review for the *Academy* mentioned above, lamented Eliot's 'preference for technical terms in lieu of the common dialect'.

Saintsbury went on to pick out a number of terms favoured by Eliot; some of the briefer examples he quoted are 'coercive types', 'spiritual penetration', 'emotive memory' and 'keenly perceptive sympathetic emotiveness'. He commented:

> The technical language of psychology is as much out of place in prose fiction as illustration of its facts is inappropriate.

CONTENT

Those critics who took exception to any aspect of the content of the novels tended to think either that the plot was improbable; or that there were elements which were a little too avant-garde for them to feel comfortable with; or that some of the subject matter was inappropriate.

Plot

The endings of *Adam Bede* and *The Mill on the Floss* were judged by some to be on the melodramatic side whilst others thought the close of *Daniel Deronda* unconvincing. The development of *The Mill on the Floss* appeared ill-judged to some critics. A contributor to the *Guardian* of 25 April 1860 pointed out that there was a 'clear dislocation in the story' between the earlier portion of the novel dealing with Maggie's childhood and the later section describing her life as an independent adult, while a commentator in the *Westminster Review* had found that 'its development is languid and straggling beyond belief'. One critic writing about *Daniel Deronda* in the *Saturday Review* of 23 September 1876 objected to the number of coincidences 'which when added or rather multiplied together make up a very unlikely whole'.

Avant-garde

Although it might seem difficult for present day readers to appreciate, some contemporary critics found aspects of Eliot's novels a little too modern for their taste. Thus the contributor to the *Saturday Review* of 26 February 1859 baulked at the unwarranted degree of biological detail provided about Hetty's pregnancy in *Adam Bede*. He felt that the novel gave him too much information about 'the several stages that precede the birth of a child'. A reviewer to the same publication, writing about *The Mill on the Floss* on 14 April, 1860, disapproved of the fact that Eliot, like Charlotte Brontë, tended to 'linger on the description of the physical sensations that accompany the meeting of hearts in love'. He had clearly been deeply unsettled by the passage in which Eliot describes Stephen covering Maggie's arm with kisses:

> There is nothing wrong in writing about such an act, and it is the sort of thing that does sometimes happen in real life; but we cannot think that the conflict of sensation and principle raised in a man's mind by gazing at a woman's arm is a theme that the female novelist can touch on without leaving behind a feeling of hesitation, if not repulsion, in the reader.

A reviewer of the same novel, writing in the *Guardian* of 25 April 1860 felt the same distaste. He applied the words 'perverted' and 'unwholesome' to the Maggie/Stephen relationship.

* * *SUMMARY* * *

- Eliot's characters were greeted with enthusiastic relish because they were so refreshingly believable although there was some low-key criticism of male characters.

- Contemporaries enjoyed the descriptions of rural life and Eliot's wit and wisdom.

- However, some critics felt there was too much authorial intrusion and that this hampered both plot and character development.

- There were some objections to Eliot's tendency to scientific language in her later novels.

- Both the plotting and the avant-garde nature of some of the content came in for criticism.

Modern Criticism

8

ELIOT'S INITIALLY WAVERING REPUTATION

Eliot's reputation during her lifetime took a downturn almost immediately after her death, aided ironically by Cross's biography. In the early part of the twentieth century, her popularity sank further because at this time the conventions of the omniscient narrator and the realist novel were regarded as hopelessly unfashionable.

There were, however, positive voices amongst the negative criticism. Leslie Stephen's *George Eliot* (Macmillan, 1902) was something of an antidote to Cross's biography and recognized the importance of Eliot's 'width of sympathy' but like other earlier writers he continued to value the early novels most highly. His daughter, Virginia Woolf, famously remarked in her article to commemorate the centenary of Eliot's birth that *Middlemarch* was 'one of the few English novels written for grown-up people', and thus ensured that the novel was taken more seriously (*Times Literary Supplement*, November 1919). David Cecil's *Early Victorian Novelists* (Constable, 1934) was perhaps limited in some respects – like others before him he emphasized the fact that her characters suffer 'always moral conflicts'. However, he also stressed the fact that, unusually for her time, she had a 'grasp of psychological essentials which give her characters their reality'.

Eliot's reputation started picking up again with F. R. Leavis's *The Great Tradition* (Chatto & Windus, 1948). Leavis unhesitatingly valued Eliot as one of the greatest novelists. G. S. Haight contributed very significantly to her rehabilitation with his work, starting with *George Eliot and John Chapman: With Chapman's Diaries* (Yale University Press, 1940), moving on through his nine-volume edition of *The George Eliot Letters* (Yale University Press, 1954–78), his edition of *A Century of George Eliot Criticism* (Methuen, 1966) and his biography

(Oxford University Press, 1968). Barbara Hardy continued to cement Eliot's reputation with a series of excellent critiques published between 1959 and 1985.

MORE MODERN TRENDS

In recent years, academic interest in Eliot has proliferated wildly: a new reader to Eliot might feel quite justifiably overwhelmed at the plethora of possibilities. A reasonable place to start might be Graham Handley's *George Eliot* in the 'State of the Art' series (The Bristol Press, 1990). Although this does not, of course, include anything written in the last decade, it is not subtitled 'A guide through the critical maze' for nothing.

Modern literary criticism has tended to view texts through a range of different approaches. Below we will sample some of the more important ideas from four of these: **deconstructionist** ideas, **Marxist** views, **feminism** and the **psychoanalytical** approach.

DECONSTRUCTIONIST IDEAS

Whereas most criticism centres on certain themes, attitudes, ideas or patterns of words which establish coherence in a text, deconstructive criticism expects (and finds) incoherence, disunity and self-contradiction. Two of the most well-regarded essays in this field are by J. Hillis Miller. 'Narrative and History' can be found in the *English Language Review* (1974) and 'Optic and Semiotic in *Middlemarch*' in *George Eliot* ed. Harold Bloom (Chelsea House, 1986). Alternatively, the latter is reprinted as Chapter 4 in *New Casebooks Middlemarch* ed. John Peck (Macmillan Press, 1992).

KEYWORDS

Deconstructionist ideas focus on the self-referential aspects of language. Jacques Derrida, whose philosophical ideas were a major influence here, showed that any text may hold a plurality of meanings and that the rhetoric of both the text and literary criticism is inherently unstable.

Marxist views focus on issues around class and power.

Feminism is the study of gender politics from a female perspective.

Psychoanalytical criticism may look at how far characters are motivated by subconscious desires or may develop a psycho-analytical critique of the text.

Delighting in the contrary aspects of a text, in 'Narrative and History', Hillis Miller highlights the ways in which Eliot presents beliefs and illusions which are simultaneously undermined in the novel. For instance, several characters have quite unrealistic romantic ideas about love and they sadly come to recognize that these are misconceptions. Hillis Miller then argues that history, despite being a kind of framework for events of the novel, which purports to have a historian as narrator, is actually nothing more than an 'illusion' which events of the novel debunk.

'Optic and Semiotic in *Middlemarch*' examines metaphorical patterns, in particular those involving seeing, streams and webs. Hillis Miller is interested in the ways in which these interact and in the complexity of their effects. He points out that although the omniscient narrator generalizes and attempts to present a sweeping overview, this is contradicted by the multiplicity of egocentric visions of all the different characters in the text. Moreover, whilst metaphors involving streams and webs suggest flow and interactive connectedness, this is undermined by the optical metaphors which underline the problems of perception. The trouble with language is that it cannot be definitively pinned down – Hillis Miller also quotes from *The Mill on the Floss* to show that in this novel, too, Eliot recognizes that metaphor, viewpoint and language are unreliable and shifting: 'figurative language' cannot 'make a complete, and completely coherent, picture of human life'.

MARXIST APPROACHES

As we have seen, early critics were, on the whole, delighted with Eliot's portrayal of working-class life. However, more modern critics, particularly those of a Marxist persuasion, have not wholly shared this enthusiasm.

Terry Eagleton

Terry Eagleton, in Chapter 4 of *Criticism and Ideology* (New Left Books, 1976) casts light on several of Eliot's major novels through a Marxist lens. Eagleton senses Eliot's dilemma: on the one hand, she has rural roots herself and values straightforward country folk such as those who surrounded her as she grew up. On the other hand, her impatience with their small-minded bigotry impelled her to escape – and as a novelist she feels the need to apologize 'with a blend of genial patronage and tentative irony' for making such ordinary people the main characters in novels that she presents as 'serious fiction'. The fundamental ambiguity of Eliot's stance creates difficulties for her as she writes and she tries to solve these in different ways in different novels.

Eagleton argues that in *Adam Bede*, Eliot 'tries for a partial solution of this dilemma by romantically idealizing the common life in the figures of Adam and Dinah'. Although Adam is characterized by intransigently rigid views at the beginning of the novel, he becomes humanized by his sufferings in the novel and can therefore be rewarded by marriage to Dinah Morris at the end of it. Eagleton sees Arthur Donnithorne and Hetty Sorrel as representatives of 'liberal individualism' – but rather unsatisfactory ones, as they are such unquestionably egocentric personalities, only interested in pleasing themselves. Hetty 'has unwittingly ruptured the class-collaboration between squire and artisan, turning Adam against Arthur; but once she is, so to speak, deported from the novel, that organic allegiance can be gradually reaffirmed'.

However, this same solution does not work for *The Mill on the Floss* because changes in the rural community make it less easy to idealize. There is also the difficulty that 'whereas *Adam Bede* divided moral fervour and restless individualism between Dinah and Hetty, Maggie Tulliver combines both; and this forestalls the simple resolution available to the earlier novel'.

Maggie, like Hetty, is tempted to kick against the traces of convention and to please herself – but like Dinah she has strong principles. A further problem for Maggie, in Eagleton's view is that Stephen Guest, 'the only alternative commitment which the book allows' is a decided dead end; he is 'an over-bred product of the predatory capitalism which is ousting the old rural world of her father'. Eagleton sees the end of the novel as 'transparently engineered': 'Maggie's self-sacrificial drowning with her brother suppresses ideological conflict by the magical stratagem of a literary device.'

Eagleton pays tribute to the achievements of *Middlemarch* but he finds some aspects of the novel disappointing. He points out that despite being set in a period of important historical transition, that of the Reform Bill, the novel is far more concerned with ethical decisions of a personal nature: '*Middlemarch* works in terms of egoism and sympathy, "head" and "heart", self-fulfilment and self-surrender'. Against this, the setting fades into insignificance and becomes 'more of a historical vacuum'. The kind of solid rural values which *Adam Bede* presented are incarnated in a more peripheral character, Caleb Garth. High ideals and visions collapse at the close of the novel and characters end up settling for more low-key, less ambitious achievements.

Eagleton recognizes that Will Ladislaw is a more romantic and idealistic figure than other characters in the novel but that his achievements are limited by history – the Finale tells us that his zeal has been 'much checked in our days'. He points out that the hero in *Daniel Deronda* has a similar personality – but that in this novel Daniel's Jewish inheritance provides not only a romantic element but also a solid cultural identity. However, he criticizes the fact that the plot is held together by a quite improbable degree of coincidence and contrasts this artifice with the realism of *Middlemarch* where such devices are sparingly used.

Focus on representation

Simon Dentith, in *George Eliot* (Harvester Press, 1986), quotes Eliot's narrator in *Adam Bede* making a plea for the kind of social inclusion in fiction which would allow a sympathetic and true to life picture of 'old women scraping carrots with their work-worn hands, those heavy clowns taking a holiday in a dingy pothouse'. He goes on to comment on the hypocrisy of this statement, pointing out that although the words are sweepingly all-inclusive, the actuality of the writing is not:

> It is certainly not to carrot-scraping women or heavy clowns that we are most drawn in *Adam Bede*, or for that matter in any of George Eliot's novels. Indeed, she finds it persistently difficult to represent such people sympathetically, finding their 'stupidity' and resistance to higher motives, however explicable, a heavy clog on the onward processes of social life.

Dentith goes on to point out that despite the narrator's declaration that Adam had 'the blood of the peasant in his veins', Eliot deals with 'classes decidedly more respectable' than this in actuality.

However, Brian Spittles, in *George Eliot: Godless Woman* (Macmillan, 1993), argues that this is not, perhaps, so much hypocrisy or a failure of realism so much as an inaccurate use of language. He claims that Eliot uses the word 'peasant' to cover a gamut of agricultural workers from the poorest to small farmers. Spittles goes on to show how in *Middlemarch* Eliot satirizes middle-class aspirations, pointing out that *Middlemarch* deals extraordinarily perceptively with the subtleties of relationships within this level of society. He also provides a useful reminder that we, as readers, will need to understand the nuances of social difference within the strata of the middle-classes in order to appreciate this satire fully.

Class and gender

Margaret Homans, in her article 'Dinah's Blush, Maggie's Arm: Sexuality in George Eliot's Early Novels' (*Victorian Studies*, Vol. 36, no. 2, 1993) and Elizabeth Langland in *Nobody's Angels: Middle-Class Women and Domestic Ideology in Victorian Culture* (Cornell University Press, 1995) both tackle class and gender in Eliot.

Homans sees *Adam Bede* as presenting an 'image of the middle-class family triumphant' at a point in time before the middle classes were deemed to have existed. She also detects a kind of bias in the fact that 'the narrative, which lingers at Adam's workplace and dwells lovingly, too, on the hand spinning that still goes on at the Poysers', never details that determinant of Dinah's lower and more distinct class position.' She suggests that this is because 'factory spinning, in contrast to the unmodernizable building trades, is part of the threatening modernity from which Eliot seeks to protect her idealized image of the middle classes'. Homans also objects to the fact that 'the narrative humiliatingly and sentimentally dwells upon Dinah's obsession with housework' towards the end of the novel, quoting the passage which describes Dinah's particularly efficient activity with the duster to prove her point.

Langland complains that Eliot omits from her novels any reference to relationships between masters or mistresses and their servants. She also feels that Eliot fails to award her middle-class women the degree of social power that they actually had. Giving *Middlemarch* as an example, she argues that whilst Eliot appears to be critical of a world dominated by patriarchs like Brooke and Bulstrode, her heroines are too ineffective and lacking in education to take command in the wider world. Langland also restates the feminist complaint that Eliot's heroines are denied the sort of opportunities for fulfilment which their author enjoyed: she would like to see Eliot present as fictional heroine a more educated, ambitious and high achieving woman – of the sort she herself was. Other critics have challenged the inherent flaw in this anachronistic view of how a writer should perform.

FEMINIST CRITICISM

Eliot awards mediocre lives to her heroines

Kate Millett was one of the first to express this objection in *Sexual Politics* (Doubleday and Co., 1970). It is particularly well expressed by Zelda Austen in the opening of her article 'Why Feminist Critics are Angry with George Eliot' (*College English*, February 1976):

Feminist critics are angry with George Eliot because she did not permit Dorothea Brooke in *Middlemarch* to do what George Eliot did in real life: translate, publish articles, edit a periodical, refuse to marry until she was middle-aged, live an independent existence as a spinster, and finally live openly with a man she could not marry.

Of course, this irritation extends beyond *Middlemarch* – and even some Victorian readers felt disheartened by the sense of wasted potential in Eliot's heroines (see Contemporary criticism p. 60) This feeling is still being expressed by the most recent critics writing on Eliot: Kate Flint, in an essay printed in *The Cambridge Companion to George Eliot* (CUP, 2001), refers to Romola's acquiescent return to her husband after her courageous decision to leave as 'one of the more disheartening moments in all of Eliot's writing'.

But is this intentionally subversive?

Another way of looking at this problem is to see Eliot's low-key endings for her heroines as being consciously false and intentionally subversive. Kristin Brady, in *George Eliot* (Macmillan, 1992) takes this line. She deals with the endings of several novels, but is particularly interesting on *Middlemarch* when she deals with Lydgate's rather condescending attitude towards women. She points out that although the reader can sympathize with him once he realizes the true nature and limitations of the woman he has married, we also recognize that he is getting what he deserved. Moreover, this is particularly satisfying because he is mastered by a woman who uses her subordinate position as a way of getting him to behave in the way she wants. This view follows on from Gilbert and Gubar's earlier *The Madwoman in the Attic* (Yale University Press, 1979) which judged Rosamond to be George Eliot's 'most important study of female rebellion'.

Brady too is dissatisfied with the low-key life finally awarded not only to Dorothea but also to her supposed daughter. (Brady infers that of Dorothea's two children the younger was a girl.) She argues that the last sentence of the penultimate paragraph is 'the Finale's darkest statement', that this includes an implied reference to Dorothea's daughter and that the narrator's use of 'we' implies strong criticism of the trite self-sacrificial romantic fate deemed appropriate for women.

Brady also examines Mary Garth's marriage, making many thought-provoking observations. She sees Mary's choice of Fred as indicative of Mary's need to have a relatively weak husband so that she can dominate him. She also points out that Mary's younger siblings, Ben and Letty, follow the path of Dorothea's two children and are there to draw attention to the unsatisfactory and unfair treatment of intelligent females:

> The unmitigated frustration of Letty in the midst of the Finale's happy closure, like similar instances of discordance in the conclusions of Eliot's earlier fictions, … serves not only to modify the reader's sense of satisfaction but also to draw attention to the very assumptions and ideologies that underlie the romance plot and its conventional fulfilment.

A more moderate view

Other women writers have taken a more moderate position. Zelda Austen, with whom we began, is one of these. She argues that 'feminist criticism, with its call for aspiring and achieving women' is actually limiting rather than liberating. The reason why 'George Eliot could not allow Dorothea to do what she had done' was 'because she was a genius, one in a thousand, and Dorothea was not'. We should be grateful for the fact that 'George Eliot performed a service for women which ought to gain her the feminists' admiration and love rather than resentment' – she 'understood perfectly the limitations placed on women' and presented to us with sympathy and clarity 'the pain of other souls'.

Gillian Beer takes another more moderate view. In *George Eliot* (Harvester Press, 1986), she points out that Eliot's heroines are, understandably, confined within 'ordinary possibility' and that 'in *Middlemarch* particularly, she brooded on the curtailment of women's lives in terms drawn from' the women's movement 'and in sympathy with it'. In *Darwin's Plots* (CUP, 2000), Beer points out that when Gwendolen is 'taken out of the edge of the plot, out of the marriage market, out of the ordering of inheritance' in *Daniel Deronda* then: 'this is as far as her freedom can go – but for a George Eliot novel, it is a long way'.

PSYCHOANALYTICAL CRITICISM

Critics have found *The Mill on the Floss* a particularly rich ground for psychological interpretation. The very different readings tend to concentrate on language in the novel and often try to explain how the ending, which has sometimes appeared contrived to critics, has, in fact, a dreadful inevitability.

David Smith, in 'Incest Patterns in Two Victorian Novels' (*Literature and Psychology*, summer, 1965), develops the theory that an 'unconscious incestuous passion' lies behind events in the novel, and is 'a pervasive theme' – and accounts for its end. He sees 'the special feeling of Mr Tulliver for his sister Gritty' as one element here, but concentrates mainly on 'the Edenic imagery' surrounding the relationship between Tom and Maggie. His interpretation of sexuality in the language is interesting. This, he feels, has its natural culmination at the end of the novel when 'the passionate death in this scene is structurally equivalent with the passionate "death" of the sexual orgasm ... since the death is not single but joint, and the parties are clasped in an embrace, the posture of sexual union.'

In 'The Power of Hunger: Demonism and Maggie Tulliver' (*Nineteenth Century Fiction*, September 1975), Nina Auerbach sees the association of Maggie with animal imagery and her 'alliance with trees' as suggestive of her witch-like qualities. Then the fact that water is 'an element that follows Maggie and shapes her life' is particularly appropriate as 'the origin of the English ducking ritual places the witch in a typically ambiguous relationship to water'. Auerbach also links some of Maggie's behaviour to that of a vampire's. In this reading, the heroine, who has been closely associated with supernatural powers, exerts these in the novel's closing moments: Maggie 'lures Tom out of the house where he has found temporary protection ... he falls under Maggie's spell, rows the boat into the dangerous current, clings to her, and sinks, a devotee at last'.

Maggie lures Tom out of the house.

Like David Smith, Eva Fuchs, in her essay 'The Pattern's All Missed: Separation/Individuation in *The Mill on the Floss* (*Studies in the Novel*, winter, 1987) sees the spectre of unconscious incestuous feeling to be behind the ending of the novel. She examines images of fabric in the novel and looks carefully at the theme of mothering. She contrasts all those characters who have unsatisfactory mothers with Bob Jakin, who is not deprived in this respect and has, as a consequence, a much healthier sexuality. She feels that the scene in which Maggie holds Bob's baby daughter is suggestive of a promising new start:

The baby who has her name … represents her own emergent self … By imagining the death of the old Maggie who is dominated by incestuous longings and by the unsatisfied hungers of the past, George Eliot makes it possible for the new Maggie fathered by Bob Jakin to be born.

* * *SUMMARY* * *

- Interest in Eliot lapsed after her death but her reputation was rehabilitated by Leavis.

- J. Hillis Miller brings a deconstructionist perspective to Eliot.

- Terry Eagleton's Marxist views stimulated much criticism focused on issues of ideology. Later writers have concentrated on the question of whether Eliot wrote about 'peasants', as she claimed, or about the middle classes.

- Feminist criticism divides into those disappointed with the low-key fates awarded to Eliot's heroines, those who think her endings intentionally false and subversive, and those who think that Eliot was merely mirroring the fate of the vast majority of women in Victorian England.

- Psychoanalytical criticism has tended to use psychoanalytical theory to explain the ending of *The Mill on the Floss*.

Where to Next?

9

If your interest has been captured by Eliot, you may find one of the most rewarding ways of following this up is simply to read and re-read her novels, all of which seem to become richer with each new visit. If you are curious to pursue other lines of enquiry, then you might find Eliot's short story, 'The Lifted Veil' of interest. Then there is the *Impressions of Theophrastus Such*, her poems, letters, articles, and interesting websites to access.

TRY 'THE LIFTED VEIL'

Opinions of 'The Lifted Veil' have been varied since publication. To Eliot's publisher, John Blackwood, it seemed a somewhat lurid aberration: on receipt of the manuscript, he wrote to the author (and one cannot help but detect a monumental effort at understanding), 'I think you must have been worrying and disturbing yourself about something when you wrote it.'

The story is interesting, however, simply because of its difference from Eliot's usual style. In his biography of Eliot, Haight mentions that it can be seen as a forerunner of the **stream of consciousness** technique, which he sees as giving it 'a curiously modern quality', *George Eliot: A Biography* (Oxford University Press, 1968). More recent writers have developed particular and fascinating theories based on the text. Two which you might find worthwhile to refer to are Terry Eagleton's 'Power and Knowledge in "The Lifted Veil", in *Literature and History* (Vol. 9, 1983) and Jane Wood's 'Scientific Rationality and Fanciful Fiction' in *Women's Writing* (Vol. 3, 1996).

KEYWORD

Stream of consciousness is a device which describes the flow of thoughts and feelings passing through the mind of a character. It is sometimes also called 'interior monologue'. James Joyces's *Ulysses* and Virginia Woolf's *To the Lighthouse* are well-known representatives of this technique.

IMPRESSIONS OF THEOPHRASTUS SUCH

Impressions of Theophrastus Such is another work which is well worth investigating, although it has again puzzled readers. The original Theophrastus (c. 370–288 BC) was one of Aristotle's students. He wrote a series of thirty sketches of different types of people from Athens. Eliot's work, although it relies on this, is more than a series of sketches: it is a work in which she considers how fictional characters are created and how a text can be constructed by successive generations of readers. A useful edition of this text is that edited and with an introduction and notes by Nancy Henry (Pickering and Chatto, 1994).

POETRY

During her literary career, Eliot published a considerable amount of poetry, her most sustained work being *The Spanish Gypsy*. Whilst this sold well when published, it is perhaps less likely to appeal to a modern reader: Eliot said to Blackwood that he would need to prepare himself with 'fortitude' for reading it – although she was actually anticipating his possible disappointment at receiving a poem rather than a novel here.

More interesting, perhaps, are the eleven 'Brother and Sister' sonnets which Eliot wrote in 1869. She recalls the strength of her childhood relationship with her brother Isaac in these: one cannot fail to be touched by the poignancy of the evocation. You may find it interesting to compare feelings and ideas in these sonnets with the early part of *The Mill on the Floss*.

LETTERS AND ARTICLES

Haight's edition of Eliot's letters (Yale University Press, 1954–78) is an indispensable adjunct to serious study of Eliot. Not only does Haight let Eliot and her correspondents speak for themselves without bias or editing, his footnotes and commentary are invaluable.

The essays which Eliot wrote during her work on the *Westminster Review* give useful insights into her views and opinions. Some, like her often quoted 'Silly Novels by Lady Novelists' are also witty and entertaining. Thomas Pinney's edition of the *Essays of George Eliot* (Routledge & Kegan Paul, 1963) is the best way to access these.

ACCESS ELIOT ON THE WEB

Information available on the web is changing all the time, so it is a little difficult to be prescriptive here. However, I would recommend that you start with Alex Measday's site 'The Wit and Wisdom of George Eliot': http://www.geonius.com/eliot/. This will provide you with quotations from Eliot's works – but perhaps more importantly, with valuable links to other very varied sites.

One link is to that of Mitsuharu Matsuoka's site, which Measday refers to as 'The Definitive Eliot Site' (the address is: www.lang.nagoya-u.ac.jp/~matsuoka). But there are other links which may be of particular interest if you are focused on one particular novel. For instance, Adrian Fox's English Literature Page is the place to go if you need further information on *The Mill on the Floss*, and there is a site specifically on *Middlemarch*. This gives not only a biography of Eliot but also the publication history of the novel and full details of its contemporary critical reception with a great many quotations from reviews published in newspapers and periodicals. Another link is to the journal of George Eliot-George Henry Lewes Studies. E-texts of Eliot's works are available.

JOIN A SOCIETY

One of the links from Measday's website allows you to access the George Eliot Fellowship, which you might like to join. The secretary is: Mrs Kathleen Adams, 71 Stepping Stones Road, Coventry CV5 8JT.

VISIT PLACES CONNECTED WITH ELIOT

There is no specific collection of Eliot memorabilia. Although Arbury Hall, once owned by her father's employer, is open to the public, one cannot visit any house in which Eliot lived. However, two of the London houses in which Eliot resided are now distinguished by blue

English Heritage plaques and can be viewed from the outside: 4, Cheyne Walk, SW3 and Holly Lodge, 31 Wimbledon Park Road, SW18. Brookbank, the house which she rented in Shottermill, Haslemere, and The Heights, the country home which Eliot and Lewes bought in Witley, Surrey, can again be viewed from the exterior. The latter is in Brook Road and is now a residential home called Surrey Heights.

READ MORE ABOUT ELIOT

Eliot was a fascinatingly complex personality who led a particularly interesting life for a woman of her time. You could try one of the excellent modern biographies of her such as that by Kathryn Hughes (Fourth Estate, 1999) or Rosemary Ashton (Penguin Books, 1997). If you then feel intrigued by her married life, find out more by reading the relevant section of *Parallel Lives: five Victorian Marriages* by Phyllis Rose (Knopf, 1983). Browse through the further reading list in this book for ideas for critical study.

GLOSSARY

Deconstructionist ideas focus on the self-referential aspects of language. Jacques Derrida, whose philosophical ideas were a major influence here, showed that any text may hold a plurality of meanings and that the rhetoric of both the text and literary criticism is inherently unstable.

Diegesis means a narrative account, in this case by the omniscient narrator.

An **eponymous** protagonist, from the Greek, 'giving his name to', is one who gives his or her name to the title of the work. Other examples from Eliot are *Adam Bede* and *Daniel Deronda*.

Feminism is the study of gender politics from a female perspective.

Free indirect speech (sometimes the words 'style' or 'discourse' are used rather than 'speech') is when a fictional character's thoughts and ideas are presented in the kind of vocabulary we would expect them to use themselves but are recorded in the third rather than the first person singular. Ironic ambiguity can be created when it is not entirely clear whether the author is at one with, or at an ironic distance from, the fictional creation.

Marxist views focus on issues around class and power.

Metaphorical language employs a figure of speech in which one thing is described in terms of another. For instance, in *Adam Bede*, Hetty's feelings of abandonment and isolation on her lover's departure are conveyed thus: 'She was all alone on her little island of dreams, and all around her was the dark unknown water where Arthur was gone.'

Mimesis – from the Greek *mime*, to imitate, meaning to represent the truth. A character is behaving or speaking in a way which is convincingly life-like.

An **omniscient** narrator is one who is seemingly in the position of knowing everything – from the Latin, *omnes* – all.

Psychoanalytical criticism may look at how far characters are motivated by subconscious desires or may develop a psychoanalytical critique of the text.

The word **realism** is much used in literary criticism: it is a somewhat elastic term. It is probably most helpful to think of its meaning life as lived by recognizably ordinary people – and the complete opposite of the unreal or fantastic.

Stream of consciousness is a device which describes the flow of thoughts and feelings passing through the mind of a character. It is sometimes also called 'interior monologue'. James Joyces's *Ulysses* and Virginia Woolf's *To the Lighthouse* are well-known representatives of this technique.

Chronology of major works

1846 Publication of Eliot's translation of Strauss's *The Life of Jesus, Critically Examined*.

1854 Publication of Eliot's translation of Feuerbach's *The Essence of Christianity*, the only book of hers published under the name 'Marian Evans'.

1855 Writes and publishes articles for the *Westminster Review*.

1858 *Scenes of Clerical Life* published.

1859 *Adam Bede* published in three volumes; 'The Lifted Veil' published in *Blackwood's Edinburgh Magazine*.

1860 Marian Evans recognized as 'George Eliot' – although *The Mill on the Floss* is, like all later novels, published under the pseudonym.

1861 *Silas Marner* published.

1862 *Romola* (1863) serialized in the *Cornhill Magazine*.

1866 *Felix Holt, The Radical* published.

1867 *The Spanish Gypsy* published.

1871 Serialization of *Middlemarch* begins in December with the first book.

1872 The remainder of *Middlemarch* appears in serialized form.

1873 *The Legend of Jubal and Other Poems* published.

1876 *Daniel Deronda* published.

1879 *Impressions of Theophrastus Such* published.

FURTHER READING

Biography

Haight, G. S. *George Eliot: A Biography* (Oxford University Press, 1952)

Hughes, Kathryn *George Eliot* (Fourth Estate, 1998)

Criticism

Austen, Zelda 'Why Feminists are Angry with George Eliot' (*College English*, 37, 1976)

Beer, Gillian *Darwin's Plots: Evolutionary Narrative in Darwin, George Eliot, and Nineteenth-Century Fiction* (Cambridge University Press, 2000); *George Eliot* (Harvester Press, 1986)

Bloom, Harold *George Eliot* (Chelsea House, 1986)

Brady, Kirsten *George Eliot* (Macmillan, 1992)

Dentith, Simon *George Eliot* (Harvester Press, 1986)

Gilbert, Sandra M. and Susan Gubar *The Madwoman in the Attic* (Yale University Press, 1979)

Haight, G. S. (ed.) *A Century of George Eliot Criticism* (Methuen, 1966)

Handley, Graham *George Eliot: A Guide Through the Critical Maze* (The Bristol Press, 1990)

Hardy, Barbara *The Novels of George Eliot* (Athlone Press, 1959)

Hillis Miller, J. 'Narrative and History', *English Language Review* (1974)

Homans, Margaret 'Dinah's Blush, Maggie's Arm: Sexuality in George Eliot's Early Novels', *Victorian Studies* (Vol. 36, No. 2, 1993)

Levine, George *The Cambridge Guide to George Eliot* (Cambridge University Press, 2001)

Peck, John   New Casebooks *Middlemarch* (Macmillan Press, 1992)

Spittles, Brian   *George Eliot: Godless Woman* (Macmillan, 1993)

Turner, Mark and Levine, Caroline   editors of the Special Number 'Gender, Genre and George Eliot', *Women's Writing* (Vol. 3, No. 2, 1996)

Collections of Eliot's letters and essays

Haight, G. S.   (ed.) *The George Eliot Letters* (Yale University Press, 1954–78)

Pinney, Thomas (ed.)   *The Essays of George Eliot* (Routledge & Kegan Paul, 1963)

INDEX